SHIH TZU

JENNY DRASTURA

Shih Tzu

Editor: Heather Russell-Revesz
Indexer: Dianne L. Schneider
Designer: Mary Ann Kahn

TFH Publications®
President/CEO: Glen S. Axelrod
Executive Vice President: Mark E. Johnson
Editor-in-Chief: Albert Connelly, Jr.
Production Manager: Kathy Bontz

TFH Publications, Inc.®
One TFH Plaza
Third and Union Avenues
Neptune City, NJ 07753

Discovery Communications, Inc. Book Development Team: Marjorie Kaplan, President and General Manager, Animal Planet Media / Kelly Day, EVP and General Manager, Discovery Commerce / Elizabeth Bakacs, Vice President, Licensing and Creative / JP Stoops, Director, Licensing / Bridget Stoyko, Associate Art Director

Printed and bound in China

13 14 15 16   3 5 7 9 8 6 4 2

Library of Congress Cataloging-in-Publication Data
Drastura, Jenny.
  Shih tzu / Jenny Drastura.
      p. cm.
  Includes index.
  ISBN 978-0-7938-3719-9 (alk. paper)
  1. Shih tzu. I. Title.
  SF429.S64D73 2011
  636.76--dc22

                            2010052262

This book has been published with the intent to provide accurate and authoritative information in regard to the subject matter within. While every reasonable precaution has been taken in preparation of this book, the author and publisher expressly disclaim responsibility for any errors, omissions, or adverse effects arising from the use or application of the information contained herein. The techniques and suggestions are used at the reader's discretion and are not to be considered a substitute for veterinary care. If you suspect a medical problem consult your veterinarian.

Note: In the interest of concise writing, "he" is used when referring to puppies and dogs unless the text is specifically referring to females or males. "She" is used when referring to people. However, the information contained herein is equally applicable to both sexes.

The Leader In Responsible Animal Care for Over 50 Years!®
www.tfh.com

CONTENTS

ORIGINS OF YOUR
SHIH TZU

If you are reading this book, you have obviously been charmed by the little dog who has come to be known as the Shih Tzu. Described as lively, alert, proud, and arrogant, he is also silly, happy, and clownlike. So how did this beautiful dog with his long flowing coat become a part of our lives? Furthermore, how can we explain the existence of a species, the domestic dog, with so many varieties? More than 400 distinct dog breeds serve as companions, guardians, herders, hunters, service dogs, show dogs, and film stars. Yet after more than 14,000 years of domestication and natural selection by breeders for desired characteristics, the DNA makeup of dogs and wolves is almost identical.

DOG MEETS MAN

No one knows for sure how dogs became domesticated. One theory is that wolves came to campsites, attracted by the smell of food, and the tamer ones were adopted by humans who recognized the wolves for their superior tracking, hunting, and guardian skills. They assisted humans in these tasks, as well as acting as clean-up details, providing warmth, and, yes, serving as food. Early humans may have taken cubs from their dens to hand raise. Without a parent to take care of them, the cubs would have become dependent on their humans.

With their superior powers of scent, the wolf/dogs could track game and slow prey down until a human could appear with his ax or spear, and later bow and arrow. With their superior hearing, the dogs could listen for danger from wild animals and sound an alarm. It seems that these early dogs even eventually grew to recognize humans as members of their pack and learned to become part of their social hierarchy.

MAN SHAPES DOG

Certainly no other species has had such a close association with humans for so long, or has been shaped by humans as the dog has. As other animals like sheep and cattle were domesticated, early humans selected and developed herding skills in what were becoming the first true dogs. These early

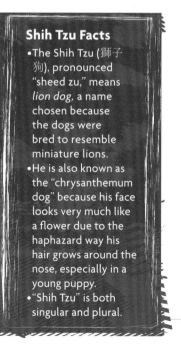

Shih Tzu Facts
- The Shih Tzu (獅子狗), pronounced "sheed zu," means *lion dog*, a name chosen because the dogs were bred to resemble miniature lions.
- He is also known as the "chrysanthemum dog" because his face looks very much like a flower due to the haphazard way his hair grows around the nose, especially in a young puppy.
- "Shih Tzu" is both singular and plural.

The Shih Tzu is a close genetic match to the Pekingese (left) and the Lhasa Apso (right).

dogs were called "landrace breeds" because they developed according to their environment and function. As duties became more specific, so did the breeds. When the wheel made its debut, dogs were used to pull carts and wagons. When humans went to war, they trained dogs for battle. Gamblers put their money on racing dogs as early as several millennia ago.

In agriculture, dogs were used to pull plows and power wheels that turned roasts over open flames. Terriers hunted vermin and other canines helped man retrieve birds, stand game, and drive cattle. More recently, dogs have been trained for search and rescue, to detect arson, and to sniff out drugs. Therapy dogs bring joy to hospitals, nursing homes, rehabilitation centers, and schools, while service dogs are trained to perform tasks for the disabled.

Dogs have been connected with primitive religious rituals going back thousands of years, for either sacrifice or veneration. Some were, or still are, revered as holy dogs, as we will see with the Asian breeds. More recent breeds are attributed to Catholic monasteries where they have been bred and trained for hundreds of years.

Toy breeds had jobs as well. In addition to the terrier toy breeds used as ratters, in ancient and medieval times some toys were carried around to ward off sickness or bear away fleas. Some were placed on the stomach or chest of the ailing for comfort or, some say, to draw out disease. Toy dogs are more than capable of acting as sentinel dogs, barking a sharp warning when friend or foe approaches.

ANCIENT BREEDS

While it is easy to trace the history and purpose of breeds developed in the past several hundred years, it is nearly impossible to be entirely sure how the ancient breeds evolved. In the early 1900s, Professor Ludwig Von Schulmuth, a noted expert in all things canine, spent a considerable time in Africa studying the skeletal remains of dogs found in human settlements as old as the Paleolithic Era (about 10,000 years ago). He created a genealogical tree of Tibetan dogs that showed that the *Gobi Desert Kitchen Midden Dog*, a scavenger, evolved into the *Small Soft-Coated Drop-Eared Hunting Dog*, which in turn evolved into the Tibetan Spaniel, Pekingese, and Japanese Chin. Another branch coming down from the *Kitchen Midden Dog* gave rise to the Papillon and Long-haired Chihuahua; yet another branched into the Pug and Shih Tzu.

Von Schulmuth placed the Lhasa Apso, Tibetan Terrier, and Tibetan Mastiff as coming from the *Large Spitz-Type Dog*, which evolved into the *Heavy-Headed Dog that Moved North*. This leads to the Ovcharka breeds of Russia and central Asia and then divides into the Mongolian branches. These branches, in turn, lead to the *North Funlun Mountain Dog* and *South Funlun Mountain Dog*, and from there to the Tibetan Terrier and Lhasa Apso.

More recently, in a study of the genetic structure of 85 breeds, the Shih Tzu, the Lhasa Apso, and the Pekingese paired off in a close relationship when the molecular markers were compared. The researchers sorted the 85 breeds into four major groups, based on genetic similarities. The fourth, or ancient, group includes 14 geographically diverse breeds that are not usually grouped together, including:

- the Chow Chow, Shar-Pei, Shih Tzu, Pekingese, Tibetan Terrier, Lhasa Apso, Akita, and Shiba Inu;
- the African Basenji;
- the Middle Eastern Saluki; and
- the Siberian Husky and Alaskan Malamute.

The Shih Tzu has served as a companion to many centuries of Tibetan and Chinese monks, emperors, and empresses.

This study, plus the historic evidence, verifies that the Shih Tzu is, indeed, a close genetic match to the Lhasa Apso and the Pekingese. Still, it is most likely that the Tibetan dogs intermixed as they do now in Tibet and China. The Chinese applied the name lion-dog (*Shih-tzu kou*) to any long-coated dog, whether native or foreign, large or small. The Lamaists themselves say they are willing to call any shaggy-coated dog a "lion-dog."

THE ORIGIN OF THE SHIH TZU

The Shih Tzu has served as a companion to many centuries of Tibetan and Chinese monks, emperors, empresses, and even us common folk. Although much of the history has been lost, we do have enough written records and artwork to give us some clues as to how the breed came about.

SMALL DOGS IN ANCIENT CHINA

The actual origin of dogs in China is scanty, in part because of the so-called "Burning of the Books" in the year 212 B.C.E. On the advice of his minister, Emperor Shih Huang-ti decreed that all books dealing with the past be destroyed. In spite of his attempts to have history begin with him, archaeologists have found evidence that "square dogs" and "short" dogs existed as far back as 1760 B.C.E. in the Hunan Province.

According to surviving records from the Chou Dynasty, (about 1027 B.C.E. to about 221 B.C.E.), the yearly tribute from the southern states consisted of amber, pearls, ivory, rhinoceros horns, kingfishers' feathers, and "short dogs." Records dated to 600 B.C.E. describe a short-mouthed dog called a "Shejo." In the 5th century B.C.E., Shejos are mentioned again as dogs that are carried, whereas a longer-mouthed type of dog followed the chariots.

Records from the first century C.E. mention several dogs, including the "hsien," a black dog with a yellow chin, and a "mang," a dog with plenty of hair. A dog who barked incessantly was called a "hsien." An "ao" was a dog that "knows man's heart." In C.E. 228 the king was presented with a "dog of five colors."

The oldest artistic representation of dogs in China is a bronze bowl from the Chou Dynasty, engraved with 100 animals, including dogs. In some cases, dogs were considered capable of warding off evil and thus were buried under the city gates to protect those inside.

During the early Han Dynasty (around 100 B.C.E.), two major trade routes carried silk to Rome and Greece in exchange for toy dogs, fighting dogs, and hunting dogs, along with other animals and treasures. Two dogs, a male and a female, matching the description of the "Melitaei," or the Roman Maltese, were presented to the Emperor Kou Tzu around C.E.620 as a gift from the Holy Roman Emperor in Byzantium. More Maltese were obtained from Muslim traders in China, making it likely that many Chinese toy dogs go back to those imports.

Some of the early dogs were called by the name "Pai," which later Chinese authorities say referred to a very small "short-legged" and "short-headed" type of dog, which belonged under the table. The Chinese table of the period was low, about eight inches (20 cm) high, and people around it sat on mats.

Ancestors of the Shih Tzu were Fu dogs—palace or temple dogs from ancient China.

FU DOGS

When Buddhism came to China around the 1st century, the symbol of the new religion was the lion. Tamed and conquered by the Buddha, the lion became his faithful servant. As the Chinese converted to Buddhism, the lion became a very common figure in their art.

As there were no lions in China, and the few sent to the Emperor did not survive, there was no living symbol of Buddha's greatness. That is, there weren't until someone discovered that the "King of the Beasts" resembled the Emperor's Fu dogs, known as palace or temple dogs. From then on, the Fu dogs were known as "lion dogs," and these are the ancestors of the Pekingese.

During the Ming Dynasty of the 14th century, the lion dog fell out of favor. The emperors worshipped cats and kept thousands of them in the palace. The cats had official ranks and titles and were fed by servants of the emperor.

APSO DOGS

When the Manchu Dynasty came into power, dogs were again in favor. In 1653, the Dalai Lama paid a visit to the Manchu emperor in Peking (now Beijing), paying tribute to the royals by presenting honey-colored dogs called "Apso" (a corruption of the Tibetan word *prapso*), meaning shaggy. These dogs were subsequently sent every year as gifts. The sending of lion-dogs to Chinese emperors by the Tibetans symbolized presentation of lions to the Buddha, who came to earth from heaven riding on a lion. In the Buddhist cycle, the spirit of man passes into the form of a dog, creating this close relationship. The dogs were considered on their spiritual journey to Nirvana, just as man was. For this reason, the lion dogs had been well-kept secrets in the Buddhist monasteries for many centuries.

The imperial family liked the dogs from the Dalai Lama and asked for more. They did get more, but, as the dogs were considered one of the most esteemed and valuable of all tributes, the Chinese did not receive as many as they would have liked. In order to perpetuate this lovely exotic dog, it is said the Chinese crossed the Apso with their own equally esteemed Palace Dogs, the Pekingese, or *Bei-jing gou*, creating what would become the Shih Tzu.

During the Manchu Dynasty in the 17th century, a Jesuit priest noted that the noble ladies played with little dogs to pass away the time. The dogs were called *Pen-Lo* (lump forehead) or *Shih Tzu Paerh* (*Lion Paerh*). They are described as very small and extremely intelligent, and could take things with their mouths and sit, beg, roll, and do other tricks.

THE EMPERORS' TREASURES

As dogs were considered treasures, they belonged to the emperor, and good fortune would come to anyone breeding dogs that pleased him. The emperors were continually followed by their small dogs, and their entrance to audiences was often announced by the barking of the accompanying dogs as a signal for all servants to hide themselves, or at least to avert their faces. Some of the dogs

Ancestors of the Shih Tzu were considered treasures of the emperor.

even held the emperor's robe and would sit and wag their tails at every audience.

For centuries, palace eunuchs were charged with the responsibility of breeding the dogs. They were inclined to experiment in hopes of producing unusual colors or features to win royal favor. Sadly, cruel measures were sometimes used to create the desired look and diminutive size. Eventually very small dogs were being bred, owing to the mixing of local dogs with small imports from other countries, such as the Maltese.

The Shih Tzu is also known as the "chrysanthemum dog" because his face looks very much like a flower, due to the way his hair grows.

Pedigrees did not exist in ancient China, but very careful breeding records were contained in the dog books of each imperial master. The highest compliment a Chinese breeder could be given was to have a specimen good enough to go into the imperial dog book. Very few of these books have been allowed to leave the palaces, but those that have been obtained portray dogs closely resembling the Pekingese, the Pug, and the Shih Tzu. The most outstanding dogs were painted by the court painters on scrolls of silk that embellished the walls of the palaces.

THE EMPRESS TZU HSI

During the time of the Empress Dowager Tzu Hsi (1861-1908), hundreds of dogs were in the imperial palace, supervised by the empress herself. An entire staff attended to the dogs, and food was selected as if for a child. Puppies were subject to her inspection, and she tried to produce certain traits by judicious breeding, such as markings and color. She objected to the cruel methods used by the eunuchs to retard growth and change facial structure. The eunuchs would sell the inferior specimens on the black market, where commoners would obtain and breed them.

During the empress's reign, dogs were raised to a height of almost religious veneration and secluded from the western world in a veil of mystery and glamour. The dogs were exercised, carried in luxurious sedan chairs, given daily baths, sprinkled with sweet-smelling perfumes, and fed the daintiest of foods. They would act as bed warmers for the emperor and empress. Heinous punishments were meted out to anyone who dared remove a dog from the palace grounds. These punishments were finally abolished in 1905 by the Dowager Empress.

In 1908, just before the Empress Tzu Hsi's death, the Dalai Lama visited her, bringing with him several Tibetan Lion Dogs. At that time, there were three types of dogs being carefully bred by the eunuchs: the Pekingese, the Pug, and the longhaired Shih Tzu. At the empress's funeral, one of her favorite dogs, Moo-Tan, a yellow and white dog with a spot on its forehead, was led before her coffin.

Following the empress's death, her breeding stock was dissipated. Many were sold by the eunuchs to Chinese noblemen or given away to foreign visitors. Bedlam ensued and palace treasures, including the empress's precious dogs, goldfish, and silkworms, were destroyed or stolen as the Boxer Rebellion of 1900 took its toll. Breeding continued outside the palace in the homes of the Chinese or foreigners. There was no registry for these dogs in China until the 1930s, and there was a great deal of confusion as to which dog was which breed. It would take several years before standards were set for these breeds.

Many breeds became nearly extinct in China and the Tibetan region during the Chinese Revolution. The surviving dogs were difficult to find, but gratefully, enough were rescued to allow us to enjoy these charming breeds as we know them today.

The American Shih Tzu Club (ASTC) was formed in 1963.

THE SHIH TZU IS INTRODUCED TO THE WORLD

A black-and-white pair of Shih Tzu, Hibou and Shu Ssa, owned by General Sir Douglass and Lady Brownrigg, were among the first of the breed to arrive in England, in 1930. At first they were classified as "parti-colored Apsos." After a ruling and much discussion by the Kennel Club (KC) in England, the Shih Tzu became a separate breed. The taller breed with the narrower head and longer nose was called the Lhasa Apso; the lower type with the round head and shorter nose was the Shih Tzu.

Lady Brownrigg (who owned the first English champion Shih Tzu, Ta Chi of Taishan), coined the name "chrysanthemum dog." She described Shu Ssa as follows:

"She was white with a black patch on her side, root of tail, and head. This had a white topknot or applemark. Her hair was not as long as it became, but it stuck up all round her face, and with her large eyes she looked like a fluffy baby owl or perhaps a chrysanthemum."

The Shih Tzu Kennel Club of England was formed in 1935 under the presidency of the Countess of Essex with Lady Brownrigg serving as secretary. In 1940, the

Kennel Club granted the Shih Tzu a separate registry, allowing the breed to become registered as purebred dogs. World War II curtailed any dog sport for the next ten years, however. In the meantime, additional dogs were searched for in China and imported into England and the rest of Europe.

THE SHIH TZU IN AMERICA

The little dogs did not go unnoticed by members of the U.S. Armed Forces who were stationed in England. They became intrigued by the dogs and brought them back to the United States. Other dogs would follow but, since they were not yet recognized by the American Kennel Club (AKC), they could not be shown or registered for breeding.

Interestingly, seven of the original Shih Tzu brought to the United States were erroneously registered with the AKC as Lhasa Apsos. Before anyone realized these dogs were actually a different breed, they had already been used extensively in many Lhasa Apso breeding programs and had finished championships. This mix-up was eventually straightened out, but the vast majority of Lhasas in the United States can trace their pedigrees to those early Shih Tzu crosses.

By 1955 there was enough interest in the Shih Tzu for the AKC to accept the breed in the Miscellaneous Class, meaning they could compete in obedience and for placements, but not for championship points. (This is the normal procedure for new breeds to determine whether there is enough of a nationwide interest and activity in the breed.) The breed gained favor very quickly, and The American Shih Tzu Club (ASTC) was formed in 1963. The AKC opened its Stud Book to the Shih Tzu on March 16, 1969. Three thousand dogs became eligible for registration as foundation stock.

On September 1, 1969, the breed was shown for the first time for championship points. When that day came, fanciers were full of excitement. Chumulari Ying-Ying, a male Canadian champion, won Best in Show over 970 dogs the very first day at the New Brunswick Kennel Club show. As far as anyone knows, no other breed has won Best in Show on its first day of eligibility. Then, after accumulating 15 points in 13 days, a male named Bjorneholms Pif became the breed's first AKC champion.

Today the Shih Tzu is one of the most popular registered breeds and has appeared in the Top 10 of AKC registrations on a regular basis.

CHARACTERISTICS OF YOUR SHIH TZU

Decades ago, breeder James E. Mumford wrote in the *American Shih Tzu News* that he had learned more about the origin of the breed from his dog, Choo Choo, than from breed historians. He put together this whimsical recipe for the Shih Tzu: "A dash of lion, several teaspoons of rabbit, a couple of ounces of domestic cat, one part court jester, a dash of ballerina, a pinch of old man (Chinese), a bit of beggar, a tablespoon of monkey, one part baby seal, a dash of teddy bear and the rest dogs of Tibetan and Chinese origin." While the background of the Shih Tzu may not be quite as diverse as that, we know from the previous chapter his origin is certainly fascinating!

Shih Tzu registered with the American Kennel Club (AKC), the largest purebred dog registry in the world, are shown in the Toy Group. They are not, however, true toys—in personality or temperament. According to longtime fanciers, the breed still has too much of the deeply ingrained dignity and reserve of its Tibetan ancestors to openly ask for or lavish affection as a toy dog would. Like the Holy Men of Tibet, your Shih Tzu will spend much time in deep meditation. Then, when he has searched his soul to his own satisfaction, he will open up and show that he can clown with the best of them.

HE'S GOT THE LOOK

Breed clubs derive standards about how a breed should look in order to give breeders and judges guidelines to determine which dogs are most suitable for breeding stock. However, no dog is perfect according to the individual breed standard—not even the greatest of champions.

SIZE

According to the American Shih Tzu Club (ASTC), the Shih Tzu is a small but solid and compact dog, ranging from 8 to 11 inches (20 to 28 cm) tall at the shoulders. Ideally, the height is 9 to 10½ inches (23 to 27 cm), and he should be slightly longer than he is tall. He should weigh between 9 and 16 pounds (4 to 7 kg). Females tend to be slightly smaller and finer-boned than males.

The Shih Tzu's double coat is long, flowing, and soft.

BE AWARE!

Beware of labels such as the "Imperial" or "Teacup" Shih Tzu. Unethical breeders have deliberately downsized the breed to create a market that profits from them but results in dogs with special medical needs, health issues, and often shorter life spans.

Going to Extremes

Though a descendant of the larger Lhasa Apso and the smaller Pekingese, the Shih Tzu is not a "designer dog" or hybrid. It took many generations of breeding and selection for the Shih Tzu to come into its own. Any extreme "version" of the Shih Tzu that does not meet the standard is simply not correct. Unethical breeders have deliberately downsized the breed to create a market to make money at the expense of undersized dogs with special medical needs, health issues, and often shorter life spans. Beware in particular of labels such as the "Imperial" or "Teacup" Shih Tzu. (However, if you already have one of these small dogs, or if your Shih Tzu is oversized or otherwise does not meet the standard, he is still more than worthy of your love and affection!)

COAT

The Shih Tzu's double coat is long, flowing, and soft, with a straight outer coat, originally to protect him from the elements. A slight wave is permissible, but the coat should not be curly or sparse. A soft, thick undercoat protects his organs and joints.

COLOR

Originally, golden-yellow was the favored coat color of the emperors, but other colors were permitted as well: solid yellow (*Chin Chia Huang Pao*), yellow dogs with a white mane (*Chin Pan To Yueh*), black-and-white dogs (*Wu Yun Kai Hsueh*), solid black dogs (*Yi Ting Mo*), and multi-colored dogs (*Hua Tse*).

Colors one might see in the Shih Tzu today are gold and white; red and white; black mask gold; solid red; black and white; solid black; solid liver; liver and white; blue and white; brindle and white; and silver and white. All coat colors are considered correct.

HEAD AND FACE

The head and expression of the Shih Tzu distinguish the breed from all others. Shih Tzu have dark, large, round eyes. The eyes should not be too small, too prominent, or close-set. Too much eye white gives the dog a startled look and is undesirable in the show ring. The Shih Tzu's facial characteristics contribute to an expression that is warm, sweet, wide-eyed, friendly, and trusting—designed to make you melt.

The rare "blue" Shih Tzu, who lacks the color gene for black, will have dilute blue or gray eyes. They also have blue pigment on the muzzle, nose, lip, footpad, and eye rims. A "liver-pigmented" Shih Tzu will have lighter brown eyes and pigment. Blue eyes are unacceptable in the show ring in any color except blue dogs. Light eyes of this kind do not affect vision or the dog's overall health. This is purely a cosmetic consideration.

Shih Tzu have dark, large, round eyes that contribute to their trusting expression.

The Shih Tzu's nose and eye rims should be black, with the exceptions mentioned above. It is considered a fault for the dog to have pink on the nose, lips, or eye rims. In contrast to the longer-muzzled Lhasa Apso or the shorter, wrinkled muzzle of the Pekingese, the Shih Tzu has a square, short, unwrinkled muzzle. It should be set no lower than the bottom eye rim and never downturned or snipey (pinched or pointed). It should be no longer than one inch (3 cm) from the tip of the nose to the stop, although length may vary slightly in relation to the overall size of dog. The nose may be straight or tilted slightly upward. If your dog's nose is tilted upward, this will add to the desired "arrogant" look.

The bite is undershot with a broad and wide jaw. Having six teeth in a straight row between the larger canine teeth is considered ideal, but a missing tooth or slightly misaligned teeth are not severely penalized in the show ring. The teeth and tongue should not show when the mouth is closed. Even less desirable is the overshot jaw, which occurs when the muzzle is too long, ruining the expression. This last characteristic goes back centuries to the preferences of the imperial court.

BODY

Structurally the Shih Tzu should be an overall well-balanced dog. Enhancing his proud look, he should have a natural high head carriage, the neck neither too long nor too short, but rather in balance with his proportions. His topline, the spinal section from the top of his shoulder blades to the end of his tail root, should be level. His chest should be broad and deep with good spring-of-rib, but not barrel-chested (with a large ribcage). Depth of the ribcage should extend to just below the elbow. The distance from elbow to withers (between the shoulder blades) is a little greater than from elbow to ground.

The tail, one of the breed's most distinguishing features, is set on high, heavily plumed, and carried in a gentle curve well over the back.

OVERALL LOOK

The Shih Tzu is a rugged, active companion dog who should be appraised on the same basis of its Himalayan ancestors—that is, well-muscled legs and a sturdy body tracing back to the native mountain environment of Tibet, where overall hardiness was the key.

Many years ago, Shih Tzu fancier The Reverend Roger A. Williams wrote:

"Look at the Shih Tzu outline as he stands proud, strong, alert, the embodiment of vigor... see him move with his massive-looking fore-paws thrusting purposefully through the long dense hair of his coat. Hindlegs flashing their pads as they drive the stead body, head carried high and tail forward, as free as a ship under full sail."

IS THE SHIH TZU FOR YOU?

The Shih Tzu appears to have taken on many of the traits of the Pekingese, possibly because they shared the same role in the temples—that of royal companion. Both of these small dogs share a sense of independence and directness. They are not dainty, but rather courageous and bold, combining a dignified regality with intelligence and affection.

According to the ASTC, the sole purpose of the Shih Tzu is that of a companion and house pet; so it is essential that the breed's temperament be outgoing, happy, affectionate, friendly, and trusting towards all. However, like many other small dogs, Shih Tzu seem to have no concept of their own size. They are "huge dogs packed into a small body." They can be so overconfident they will approach a much larger dog without a second thought, and they are quick to defend a canine friend under attack.

Like humans, dogs are individuals too, so personalities can vary. The Shih Tzu has been described as loving, loyal, brave, outspoken, and contemplative. Some bond to the entire family; others choose one family member to adhere to. They love to play, yet are happy lounging on the couch or snuggling on their own bed. They love toys and just "doing their own thing" on occasion. They are very devoted little dogs, but they will not be your servant. Your Shih Tzu will assume he is your equal, if not your superior!

ENVIRONMENT

The Shih Tzu does not need a lot of space to be happy. As much as Shih Tzu enjoyed the expansive royal palaces of China, they do make great apartment dogs. A small back yard is always a plus, but they are just as happy being walked around the neighborhood on a leash, checking out their kingdom.

Outdoors

While he enjoys the outdoors, a Shih Tzu should never be left outside on his own or, more importantly, left to roam. A secure fenced-in yard is ideal.

He should never be left out in hot weather, even if his coat is clipped short. Short-faced dogs have a high risk of heatstroke because they can't pant vigorously enough to lower their body heat. When the weather is cold—beware! He may want to stay out too long. Don't underestimate the damage the cold ground or snow can do to his feet and pads, not to mention coming in with ice balls attached to his coat. If he does play in the snow, check his pads for impacted ice when he comes in.

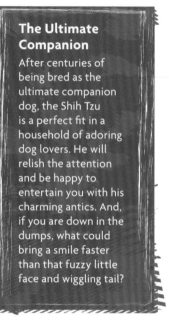

The Ultimate Companion

After centuries of being bred as the ultimate companion dog, the Shih Tzu is a perfect fit in a household of adoring dog lovers. He will relish the attention and be happy to entertain you with his charming antics. And, if you are down in the dumps, what could bring a smile faster than that fuzzy little face and wiggling tail?

COMPANIONABILITY

Since the purpose of the Shih Tzu is that of a companion and house pet, it is essential that his temperament be outgoing, happy, affectionate, friendly, and trusting towards all. Of course, there will be variations in personality based on upbringing, genetics, and training. Some Shih Tzu can be a little aloof, which recalls their royal heritage; some can appear to be a little arrogant, which just adds to their charm. However, the breed should never be aggressive or confrontational.

Shih Tzu and Children

A well-trained Shih Tzu and a well-trained child can make for a good match. Shih Tzu love to play and love attention. However, children need to understand that a dog is a living thing and deserves respect.

Teach the child to approach the puppy calmly and gently and speak softly and tenderly. Puppies are prone to play-related scratching and biting, or may nip when they are getting tired. A puppy may jump up and knock the child down, so have everyone sit on the floor to play. This is especially important in case the puppy wiggles out of the child's arms and falls to the floor. Caution the child against poking the puppy or startling him with a loud voice or sudden bang. Although the Shih Tzu is a sturdy, muscular breed for its size, he does have his limits with regard to roughhousing—any small dog could be injured by careless handling. And no matter how well behaved your child may be, a puppy and child should never be left unattended.

It is beneficial to provide your dog with a quiet retreat area where he can safely go to escape from the children or to simply be alone.

Another important consideration with small children is to make sure they know how to prevent the dog from accidently escaping through the door. Your curious Shih Tzu may run gleefully from the house with no regard for what dangers may await him.

If the child understands the dog's needs, he or she can share in the responsibilities of feeding, providing water, walking, and maybe even grooming the dog. Have the child help you keep dangerous objects such as small toys out of the reach of the dog. Taking care of and loving a dog can be the most wonderful experience of a child's young life.

Shih Tzu tend to be a happy, affectionate, and friendly breed.

Consider the age and maturity of the child or children in question before you consider a Shih Tzu or any other dog. Puppies require a lot of time, patience, and socialization. If you have a young child who already requires a lot of attention, you should ask yourself whether you will have enough time to care for a puppy as well. Consider waiting until the child is of school age, or consider adopting an older dog.

Shih Tzu and Other Pets

The happy-go-lucky Shih Tzu gets along with almost anyone, even other animals. There are always exceptions, though, especially if the dog feels threatened or dominated. The threat can come from a large dog or even a similar-sized dog. It simply depends on the nature of your Shih Tzu. (After all, he may even be the one instigating the behavior.) It is best to monitor the actions of any animals meeting each other for the first time until you are certain they will get along.

As for cats, we've all heard the expression, "Fighting like cats and dogs," but every dog will react differently to a cat. Some will become annoyed, some will become good friends, and some will ignore the cat. There are many stories of the two species lying side-by-side as best friends, unaware of that unfortunate stereotype!

The Shih Tzu does not need a great deal of exercise—he is happy to go on a daily walk on a leash with his human. He will enjoy the attention, the bonding, checking out the neighborhood, and being fussed over by strangers who will certainly become friends by the next time around. He will also be happy getting exercise by playing in his own enclosed yard.

GROOMING

Before you get a Shih Tzu, consider the breed's coat and all its maintenance.

Hypoallergenic?

Some people consider the Shih Tzu "hypoallergenic." No dog can be considered truly non-allergenic, since dander (which causes the allergic reaction) can be

Most Shih Tzu can get along happily with other pets, including dogs.

found in skin, urine, and saliva. However, the Shih Tzu's coat consists of hair rather than fur. Dogs with hair shed less, similar to humans, who lose a few hairs every day to be replaced with new ones. These dogs also have less dander. For this reason they are often classified as "hypoallergenic."

Shedding

While the breed in general does not shed a lot, females may shed a great deal of coat when they are in season. It is important to keep her dutifully brushed during this time, as matting occurs more when the hair sheds. She may also shed nine weeks later at the time when puppies would have been born had she been bred. Spaying the female will, obviously, prevent this cyclical shedding. Daily brushings can prevent the small amount of shedding that can occur.

Coat Care

The long, flowing coat of the Shih Tzu is a striking sight. However, if you wish to maintain the luxurious coat yourself, it will take work! Some individuals will require daily brushings, while others can get by with once or twice a week, depending on the coat texture. The coat on the Shih Tzu's back is parted down the middle from the shoulder to the tail set. You can put the head hair in either a casual topknot or, for more formal wear, the show topknot. (How to do topknots and other grooming procedures will be described in Chapter 5). If you don't wish to put a topknot on your dog, you'll need to make sure the hair is kept out of his eyes so as not to impair vision.

If you decide that caring for the long coat is too much work, there are several types of pet clips a professional groomer can do that look very cute and are easier to care for. If you still want to try for the long coat, the groomer may be able to guide you about brushing between visits. Be sure to take into account the cost of the trips to the groomer, which will probably be on a monthly basis.

Face Care

It is helpful to wipe the Shih Tzu's face with a damp cloth after he eats to keep the hair clean, and use a towel to keep the whiskers dry. Keeping the area around the eyes clean and dry is also helpful in preventing eye stains and mucous buildup.

TRAINING

While a quick learner, the Shih Tzu can be stubborn and perhaps a little difficult to train, but with that expressive face, he is easy to forgive. If you make his training experiences enjoyable, he will love the attention and love to learn. Be very patient and consistent and never use harsh training methods. As with any other dog, you could either cause some aggressive tendencies or lose his trust entirely.

Patience also applies to housetraining your Shih Tzu, which is covered in Chapter 7. However, with positive training methods available, you can housetrain this breed—after all, your Shih Tzu's main desire is to please you.

WATCHDOG

Like his close relatives, the Shih Tzu is an excellent watchdog. He is keen to hear strange noises and will alert you to anything out of the ordinary. Some Shih Tzu bark more than others, but in general this breed isn't yappy. Be certain that you learn to speak "Shih Tzu," as they like to talk to you in modulated throaty gurgles. Your dog may be trying to tell you something very important!

CHOOSING THE SHIH TZU OF YOUR DREAMS

Now that you know what living with a Shih Tzu is like, you can go ahead and find the puppy or dog who's right for you and your family.

PUPPY OR ADULT?

Puppies are adorable, but they are a lot of work. If you think starting "from scratch" with a new puppy may be too much, consider an adult. Many adult dogs are already housetrained (though they often need some reminders and will need to learn the new routine). Many have already lived with children, so you will know that history if needed. Adult dogs have a longer attention span—you *can* teach an old dog new tricks! And an adult dog's personality and temperament are already well established, so it may be easier to find a dog suitable to your personality and lifestyle.

Some breeders have older Shih Tzu no longer being bred and shown and would like to find them a "Forever Home." These dogs

Even with a short "puppy cut," you'll still have to devote time to grooming your Shih Tzu.

can make wonderful pets and are already socialized and ready to fit into a family. Or consider adopting an adult dog from an animal shelter or rescue organization. Shelters often have purebred dogs available. These dogs simply need a home and are a marvelous investment of your time and patience. A Shih Tzu thus acquired will bond quickly with you and shower you with gratitude and unconditional love. And, most importantly, you will be saving a life!

PUPPY POINTER

Even if you don't want a show dog, a good way to find a Shih Tzu puppy is to attend a dog show and talk to the breeders. They will be able to tell you about the breed's temperament, grooming, and other general care questions.

A MALE OR A FEMALE?

Often when you go to choose a puppy, you will fall in love with an individual, regardless of sex. This may be the best way to adopt your new puppy—the emotional attachment. There are some things to consider, though, if you are trying to choose whether to get a male or a female.

If you already have a dog, it is best to choose one of the opposite sex. Dogs of the same sex are more likely to fight than dogs of the opposite sex, and most males tend to be submissive to females. If you do choose two dogs of the same sex, two males are more likely to coexist than two females. Females tend to be pushy, wanting to be "top dog," which may potentially lead to fighting. And many people report that it is much harder to break up two females than two males.

This is not to say that the Shih Tzu is a breed known to fight—it certainly is not. However, anything can happen when hormones are involved. That is why it's important to neuter or spay your pet as soon as your vet recommends. This greatly reduces your dog's chances for various types of cancers as he or she ages, and it cuts down on undesirable behaviors such as marking and that embarrassing "humping" in both sexes. In the long run, neutered and spayed pets live longer and healthier lives.

Some dog owners say males are more loving and females are more trainable. Others say males are easier to housetrain since they prefer to "hold it" until they go outside to mark their territory, while the not-so-housetrained female seems to think it is all right to eliminate wherever she wants.

Your Shih Tzu breeder can advise you about which sex or which individual puppy to adopt. After all, the breeder has known these puppies since they were born. And the more dogs you see, the more you realize that these traits seem to be more individual-based than sex-based. So go with your heart when you pick that puppy!

HOW TO FIND A REPUTABLE BREEDER

Once you have decided you want a Shih Tzu puppy, contact the ASTC (americanshihtzuclub.org) for a list of breeders in your area. If you have a local kennel club, it may maintain a breeder directory or even have a Shih Tzu person as a member. Your vet may be able to help you, too.

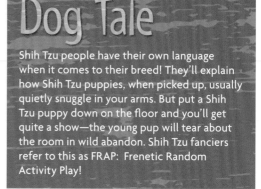

Dog Tale

Shih Tzu people have their own language when it comes to their breed! They'll explain how Shih Tzu puppies, when picked up, usually quietly snuggle in your arms. But put a Shih Tzu puppy down on the floor and you'll get quite a show—the young pup will tear about the room in wild abandon. Shih Tzu fanciers refer to this as FRAP: Frenetic Random Activity Play!

Contact the breeder early, as good breeders often have lengthy waiting lists. Visit the breeder's home to see the environment where the puppy is being raised and to see the parents, littermates, and other relatives. A reputable breeder will raise the litter at home and will have only one or two litters at one time. He or she also will not have litters from a large number of breeds. Obviously, the puppies will be clean and warm and well-fed. The mother should still be taking care of the babies if they are less than 12 weeks of age. Take the opportunity to play with the sire and dam to help ascertain their temperament. (Although you may not have an opportunity to see the sire of the litter, as he often is not owned by the breeder.)

Breeders should tell you the positive traits as well as the negative traits about their dogs. Do they tend to be smaller or larger than the average Shih Tzu? Is there a tendency toward allergies or eye problems? You will not find a single line of dogs in any breed totally free of some type of health issue. Knowing about these issues ahead of time will help you provide preventive measures, if possible, or become educated about the condition.

Be aware of so-called backyard breeders or puppy mills. There could be health or temperament problems, since these breeders do not screen out such potential issues and may not even provide good prenatal care for their breeding stock. Several important questions to separate a reputable breeder from a "backyard breeder" are:

• Have you researched genetic problems inherent in your line and in the breed?
• What kind of guarantees are included in your contract? Health and temperament?

- Are you socializing the puppies?
- Will you be available to answer questions about caring for my puppy?
- Will you take the dog back if there is a problem at some point in my life?
- Do I have to sign a contract and, if so, what will it involve?

The breeder may have questions for you, too. The breeder most likely will have certain standards of care expected from puppy buyers and will want to make sure you are the right match for the puppy. This is only fair to you and to your new family member.

RESCUE

Sadly, there are many Shih Tzu rescued every day from puppy mills or other sad situations. These dogs may require more effort to train or may have health issues, but they are just as worthy of our love and attention. If you have a warm lap and a treat to share, consider a rescue Shih Tzu.

The ASTC and regional Shih Tzu clubs have excellent rescue operations. The dogs are screened for health and temperament, are spayed or neutered, and receive the necessary veterinary care before adoption. Some clubs have a set fee and some ask for a donation to cover expenses. Many of these dogs come from kill shelters, from puppy mills, or from loving dog owners who, for whatever reason, are no longer able to care for them. Rescue dogs can end up being the most loving and affectionate dogs you will ever know, and their expressive dark eyes will "thank you" each and every day of your lives together.

Good breeders usually have waiting lists for their puppies.

SUPPLIES
FOR YOUR
SHIH TZU

One of the joys of bringing a Shih Tzu home is buying supplies. He may not appreciate it, but you know you do! The amount of money we spend on our pets just keeps on growing. And it is no longer just the traditional necessities we buy. Our purchases have extended to everything from high-end couture items to high-tech gadgets. This list of supplies includes the absolute necessities for that first day your Shih Tzu comes home, plus some optional items you might want to try.

BABY GATE

A baby gate or two is useful for keeping your Shih Tzu confined until the housetraining process is complete, or to keep him from entering a room that is not dogproof. A number of baby gates are available—but all are useful only if your dog can't climb or jump over them! Consider his athletic talents when buying a gate. The accordion-type gate can be risky if your dog tries to jump. He might catch his neck in the top of the gate and hurt himself. Gates with straight tops may be safer. Some gates use spring tension to fit various doorways, while others are permanently attached at the sides and swing open.

A clever way to protect your dog from running out the door, if you don't mind a little inconvenience, is to install a gate between your door and screen door so he will be barricaded if you need to open the door to receive a package or a pizza.

BEDS

Beds that are washable or have washable covers are the best buy. With the size of the Shih Tzu, an appropriate-sized bed should fit into a standard washing machine. There are plenty of affordable options, and, of course, there are designer beds that can be extremely pricey. Like a child, your dog may be just as happy in the box the bed came in!

CLEANING PRODUCTS

There are hundreds of commercial products to clean up after a pet, from carpet sprays to lint rollers to furniture cleaners. Enzyme cleaners modify the odor molecules and reduce odor that would draw the pup back to the same place. An ultraviolet light will light up areas you may have missed.

Yellow lawn spot removers are sold at many lawn and garden stores and home improvement

PUPPY POINTER

Never leave a new puppy alone unless he is protected in a crate or a room where he cannot get into trouble. And make sure none of his new playthings can splinter or cause a choking hazard.

A doggy rain coat can help keep your long-haired dog dry.

stores in case urine damages your lawn. If you use a commercial lawn service, check with the company to make sure they don't use any chemicals that could harm your pets.

CLOTHING

Everyone is crazy 'bout a sharp-dressed dog—or are they? There is a bit of controversy over whether dogs should be clothed.

Haute couture is not just for people anymore. Every designer from Paris Hilton to Ralph Lauren has a line of coats, sweaters, dresses, and plenty of bling for your dog. Does this mean your Shih Tzu needs to be dressed up to look like Jack Sparrow or Marilyn Monroe? That depends on how you truly wish to spend time with your dog, but, even more importantly, whether it makes the dog happy. Some dogs thrive on attention from their owners no matter how it comes. They love going to boutiques and having strangers make a fuss over them. Yet others fight even while being fitted for a basic collar.

Many dogs who suffer abuse and loneliness would love any type of attention. So find a happy medium. Spend quality time with your Shih Tzu, and if it makes him happy to slip on a little bling or some faux fur, what is the harm?

However, clothing is not always just about playing dress up. If your dog is very young, clipped down, ill, or elderly, a sweater or coat will be much appreciated in cold weather. You will appreciate a doggy rain coat in rainy weather even more when you return home with a dry long-haired dog. Your dog might really put up a fight if you try boots to keep his feet warm and dry, but sometimes they can be a plus as well.

COLLAR AND LEASH

A leash and collar are a must for your Shih Tzu's first day. He may or may not be leash trained, but he still should be secured with a collar, even if you are carrying him. Nylon collars are best for the coated breeds, as they cause the least damage to the coat. A little harder to find but even better are the rolled nylon collars for minimal coat damage. Chain-type collars are unsuitable for coated breeds because they will catch the hair and pinch the dog. Slip collars, which are made of chain or nylon and have a metal ring on each end, are not safe unless used correctly. And you can never leave a dog in a crate with such a collar—the end loop could become caught in the floor grate and choke him. Pinch or prong collars should *never* be used.

You can find quite nice matching nylon leashes at 4 feet or 6 feet (1 to 2 m) in length. I wouldn't recommend an extendable leash, as it will not give you much control and your dog can run farther than you may want him to.

Be sure when you buy that collar and leash to consider what theme you would like to convey—there are plenty of choices, including a preppy theme, a nautical theme, bones and paw prints, even seasonal collars and leashes. After all, you have a very stylish dog!

HARNESS

A harness is a good alternative to a collar, because it keeps your dog secure without choking or harming him. A typical harness conforms to the dog's body by fitting over his shoulders and under his chest, allowing for even distribution of pressure. This helps prevent choking and lessens the chance of your frisky pup's slipping out. Just make sure the harness fits correctly and does not chafe under the front legs. Some have padding for added comfort, and many harnesses are equipped to attach to your seat belt for car safety. Harnesses don't work on every dog, but many Shih Tzu do quite well with them.

CRATE

An often misunderstood but crucial item for your Shih Tzu is a crate. Crate training will be discussed in a later chapter, but it should be mentioned that a crate is not only a safe place for your dog if company comes, or service people are in your house, but also can be a private haven for your dog. His own "pad," so to speak. Dogs are den animals, and a crate can become his den when he wants some peace and quiet. If you leave the door open, chances are he will go in on his own, just to get away. If the crate will be used for a long term, you will want to get one at least twice as large as the grown dog

Harnesses are a good alternative to collars and a secure way to walk your Shih Tzu, as the dog cannot escape from them.

so there will be room for his water, bed, toys, etc., and he will not feel cramped. Using a crate properly is not cruel.

Wire or nylon mesh crates give your dog more access to his surroundings. Plastic airline-type crates offer him more privacy but may be hotter or seem confining. There are even nice wood and wicker crates that will look nice in your living room! Examine the construction of the crate and make sure your Shih Tzu's long hair will not get caught in the wire or door. Place the crate where his family will be so he will not feel isolated.

BE AWARE!
It is not safe to hold a dog on your lap in the car, particularly when you are in a seat protected by air bags. Consider using a canine car seat, crate, or dog airline bag in the back seat of your car.

Traveling will be covered in more detail in Chapter 9, but you should consider car safety. A crate or dog car harness will protect your dog during car travel. It is not safe to hold a dog on your lap in the car, particularly when you are in a seat protected by air bags. If your car has front seat air bags, keep the dog secured in the back seat.

DOGGY DOOR/BELL

Doggy doors provide a way for your pet to go outside if the yard is secured. Puppy training bells hang from your door knob so your puppy can alert you that he has to go out with the swat of a paw or the nudge of a nose.

ENTERTAINMENT

If your Shih Tzu will be staying home alone, consider entertaining him with a DVD made just for dogs. There are DVDs available that take a virtual walk through the woods, encountering various wildlife, followed by a virtual game of fetch. There are also CDs just for dogs that play relaxing music mixed with soft nature sounds and short stories, creating a peaceful environment for dogs who are left alone. Some dogs may not be happy with these sounds, though, and may want to "talk back."

EX-PEN

An exercise pen, also known as an ex-pen, is great for a dog who needs to be kept confined while you are at work or on errands. It keeps him secure and gives him plenty of room for his possessions. Ex-pens are made of metal, plastic, or PVC pipes, and come in panels. Some have small doors in one of the panels, and some require you to lift your dog out. Make sure you get one that's sturdy and tall enough. Remember James Mumsford's recipe for the Shih Tzu—a tablespoon of monkey is included in the mix. Your dog may be able to climb out of some types of ex-pens.

FENCING

Check your fence perimeter and make sure there are no holes or gaps in the fence, and make sure the gate will latch safely. If you are unable to see the gate from the door your dog will be going out, you may want to put a lock on it so no one will leave it open.

An ex-pen is great for a dog who needs to be kept confined while you are away.

FOOD BOWLS

Your Shih Tzu must have bowls for food and water. The options for decorative bowls are incredible—a long stretch from the days of the old tin or plastic bowl. You can choose from stainless steel, glass, or ceramic. If the bowl is painted, check to make sure there is no lead-based paint.

Some dogs are allergic to plastic bowls, and some health care professionals feel the plastic can harbor bacteria. If you notice an inflammation or break-out on your dog's muzzle or inside his mouth, this could be the case. But with all the other choices available, why take the risk with plastic? It's flimsy and easy to knock over.

Regardless of your choice of bowl, a doggy placemat would help lessen some spills and protect your floor, and there are a lot of cute choices available.

GROOMING SUPPLIES

Basic grooming supplies and how to use them will be discussed later, but to start out, invest in a good-quality steel pin brush and what is known as a Greyhound comb. If a Greyhound comb is not available at your pet supply store, look for a metal comb.

Hold off on bands for the hair until you can find some small latex bands like those an orthodontist would give you for braces. They are easier on the hair than ordinary rubber bands. Small fabric-covered scrunchies used for human hair also work. Note: like some humans, dogs can be allergic to latex. Although this is rare, watch out for skin irritation near where the bands are used.

Bows are a must for the well-turned-out Shih Tzu, even for the males. Doggy boutiques and web sites offer a variety of decorative bows for your Shih Tzu.

Many dog shampoos are too harsh for the human-like hair of the Shih Tzu. Buy a shampoo formulated for a coated breed or even a human hair shampoo and conditioner.

IDENTIFICATION

It is imperative that your dog have a means of identification in case he should escape from his leash or your yard.

COLLAR TAGS

A pet supply store, a vet's office, or an online service can make a metal tag that attaches to your dog's collar with everything you need to identify your dog. You should at the very least include your pet's name and your phone number on the tag.

MICROCHIP

During your first visit to the vet, request a microchip implant. The chip, which is about the size of a grain of rice, is usually implanted between the shoulder blades and can be read by a scanner. Most veterinarians and animal shelters will routinely scan any dog turned in as lost.

According to the American Kennel Club (AKC), lost pets with microchips are up to 20 times more likely to be returned home. The AKC Companion Animal Recovery (CAR) service is the nation's largest not-for-profit pet identification and 24/7 recovery service provider, using microchips for identification.

Include your pet's name and your phone number on his ID tag.

GPS

The AKC and Positioning Animals Worldwide (PAW) offer the SpotLight GPS pet locator, which couples the recovery services of AKC CAR with the tracking services provided through GPS technology. The SpotLight attaches to your dog's existing collar and has a removable, rechargeable battery. An LED beacon helps the owner locate his or her pet at night from up to 100 yards (91 m) away. An "If Found" button connects the lost dog with AKC CAR's

Recovery Team and the owner's collar tag identification. For more information about this service, visit the American Kennel Club web site at www.akccar.org.

Lap of Luxury
Shih Tzu were so highly prized by Chinese emperors they were bathed in rare perfumes and could be found lounging on beautifully embroidered silk pillows.

LICENSE

Many cities and counties require that you license your dog. The city or county will issue a tag for the dog's collar, not only to prove the dog has been registered but also to help in returning him to you. It may be a good idea to check out the local laws on dog ownership and responsibilities before acquiring your dog.

PIDDLE PADS

Depending on how you plan to housetrain your puppy or older dog, you may want to buy some piddle pads. These pads, which you place on the floor near an outside door, are made of absorbent material with a plastic bottom that protects the floor underneath. Some are scented to attract the dog.

POOP-SCOOPER

You can invest in a long-handled poop-scooper to pick up after your dog on walks. The scooper allows you to avoid having to bend over so often. If you don't want the scooper, you should at least carry some plastic bags with you when you take your Shih Tzu for a walk. It makes you a better citizen; additionally, many cities have strict laws about picking up after your dog.

SAFETY STICKERS

Some fire departments and rescue organizations provide stickers to place in your window or door to alert fire fighters and other responders to the presence of a dog or other pet in your house or apartment. This little sticker can be a lifesaver in the case of a fire or other disaster.

STROLLER

For longer walks, think about a doggy stroller with a mesh covering so your dog can see out and get plenty of air. These strollers are especially welcomed by older or infirm dogs who can no longer go for a walk with you.

TRASH CAN

Some dogs have a propensity to get into trash cans. Look for one with a lid or one that will fit under your kitchen sink to prevent both a mess and a potentially dangerous situation if your puppy should get hold of something he shouldn't eat.

TOYS

Try a pet water bottle if your dog tends to be messy with his water bowl.

Items that will make your new Shih Tzu the happiest (besides treats, of course) are toys! Not just any toy, but one that will be safe for him and give him hours of pleasure. Latex toys are a little better than vinyl, which can be chewed off in hard chunks. Plush toys are a favorite of many dogs, but monitor the play at first to make sure your dog will not disembowel the toy at the first play session. If he is a gentle chewer, a plush toy can last for years. If he's a strong chewer, look for toys recommended for busy chewers. Some toys and chews can even help keep the teeth clean.

WATER/WATER BOTTLE

Be sure your dog has access to fresh clean water at all times, but particularly at meal time. There is some evidence that the minerals in tap water could cause stains on light-colored hair, even tear stains, as the water is ingested. Therefore some people prefer to give their Shih Tzu bottled or distilled water.

A pet water bottle is another option if your dog tends to be messy with his water bowl. The bottle can be hung on the inside of the dog's crate. There are also freestanding holders for water bottles. Make sure he is able to get enough water drinking this way, however. Breeds with a tendency toward bladder stones and kidney problems should be able to drink as much water as they need.

Dog Tale

Your dog may or may not like a toy based on its color. Dogs most likely see shades of yellow gray, warm whites, blue, and blue-violet. Just for fun, I like to see whether my dogs prefer a blue or yellow toy to a red or green toy. Sometimes they only care about the noise it makes, regardless of color!

FEEDING
YOUR SHIH TZU

I n the 1860s an Ohio electrician named James Spratt was in London selling lightning rods. He happened to notice stray dogs being fed leftover ships' hardtack biscuits and other scraps. Being an inventive kind of guy, he decided he could do better with a biscuit shaped like a bone, made of wheat, vegetables, beetroot, and meat. While the formulation was based more on guesswork than science, it was clearly a step forward. His company would soon thrive selling food to English country gentlemen for their sporting dogs.

Around 1890 Spratt brought the product to the United States, where it became Spratt's Patent Limited, which eventually diversified into other feed stocks as well as veterinary medicines and pet products. Spratt's dog food was one of the most heavily marketed brands in the early 20th century. The company bought the entire front cover of the first journal of the American Kennel Club (AKC) in January 1889 to broadcast its involvement with American and European kennel clubs. In the 1950s Spratt's became part of General Mills.

Since this first venture into dog food, decades of research have been conducted in the area of canine nutrition. The types of foods available are astounding, from breed specific to disease specific, canned, bagged, dehydrated, and frozen. Some products are labeled natural or organic; they include ingredients said to promote health, such as duck, blueberries, and omega-3 fatty acids. Venison dog food is growing popular, as it is high in protein and lacks unhealthy cholesterol

So how do you choose which food is right for your Shih Tzu? And how much should you feed him?

THE BALANCED COMMERCIAL DIET

How much your adult dog eats depends on his size, age, build, metabolism, activity level, and special health issues. Dogs are individuals, just like people, and they don't all need the same amount of food. Some dogs need more fat and protein than others; some prefer canned over dry. A highly active dog will need more food than a couch potato dog, and the Shih Tzu can fall into either category. The quality of food you buy also makes a difference—the better the dog food, the further it will go toward nourishing your dog.

Most of the essential nutrients a Shih Tzu needs are required in small amounts and are present in good commercial diets, but supplements can be given upon veterinarian recommendation. We'll discuss supplementation later in this chapter.

Dog Tale

I've found that storing dog food in a seal-tight container helps prevent the food from losing its nutritional value. Mold spores or parasites could also infest the food if exposed to air.

EVALUATING DOG FOOD

By understanding a few simple concepts, you can evaluate any pet food.

As a general rule, the fewer ingredients listed in the food, the healthier it is. Foods with long lists of ingredients contain more chemicals and byproducts. Foods with fewer ingredients contain more natural nutrients and usually higher-quality meat.

The Association of American Feed Control Officials (AAFCO) is responsible for regulating the production, marketing, and sales of pet foods. Its regulations require that the labels contain the following information:

• Product name
• Net weight
• Name and address of the producer
• Guaranteed analysis
• The words "dog food"
• A statement of nutritional adequacy
• A statement of the methods used for substantiating nutritional adequacy

The AAFCO statement contains three important points to consider:

1. Whether the food is complete and balanced. "Complete" implies that the food contains all of the required nutrients for canine health in the proper amounts and ratios.
2. Which life stage of the dog the food is intended for. Only three life stages are recognized by AAFCO: adult, growth, and reproduction.
3. Substantiation of the first two claims. AAFCO regulations allow only one of two methods for supporting the claim that a food is complete and balanced for a particular life stage: analysis using laboratory or computer-based models and analysis using feeding protocols involving giving the food to living dogs under specific conditions.

Even with these points, there are problems with interpretation. If one particular product in a manufacturer's line was tested and found to meet this standard, the company is allowed to include this same statement on other products in the same family that provide equal or greater concentrations of all the nutrients. So even if the pet food carries this AAFCO food trial statement on its label, you cannot be sure that that specific product was actually tested in a food trial. Also, the food is tested in adult dogs for six months and in puppies for ten weeks. This may not be adequate time to determine whether deficiencies or other long-term effects may occur after feeding the product a year or more.

Don't just buy the cheapest brand of food. Pet food companies that produce cheap foods don't have adequate funding for proper testing of their product. You won't end up saving money in the long run.

DECIPHERING THE LABEL

Here's how to decipher what's listed on the food label:

A high-quality commercial food may be best for your Shih Tzu.

- Ingredients must be listed by weight in descending order. If meat is listed first, technically the food contains more meat than any other ingredient. In reality, chicken is a heavy ingredient because it contains a lot of water, so it's easy for manufacturers to manipulate the label by listing chicken first and following it with various grains. Companies can also separate variations of a single ingredient, such as a grain, so they can be split up and appear further down the list. This makes the food look like it has less grain than it actually does. For example, a dog food may have kibbled wheat, wheat flour, and wheat bran listed in different areas—the total amount of wheat would make it the most prevalent ingredient, but because they are split up the amount of wheat does not seem to be so great.
- The meat ingredient on the label should always be a meat with a name. For example, "chicken," "lamb," or "beef" as opposed to generic "meat." The ingredient list can be used only to determine whether the main components of a food are of animal or plant origin.
- A food should have more meat protein than grain protein.
- One or more types of meat, or high-quality dairy products such as eggs, should be listed among the first three to five ingredients. If the first ingredient is a meat, followed by grains alone, or if the first ingredient is a grain, check out other brands.
- Preservatives, artificial colors, and stabilizers in pet food must either be approved by the FDA or be generally recognized as safe. Manufacturers do not always list preservatives in ingredients like fish meal or chicken not processed by them. Preservatives can be synthetic or natural. Synthetic preservatives, such as BHA (butylated hydroxyanisole), BHT (butylated hydroxytoluene), and ethoxyquin, stop fats from turning rancid and can keep dry dog food fresh for about a year. Their safety has been questioned by some consumers and scientists, but according to the FDA they are safe at the level used in dog food. However, some manufacturers no longer use these synthetics, preferring natural preservatives like vitamin E (mixed tocopherols), vitamin C (ascorbic acid), and

extracts of various plants such as rosemary. Natural preservatives keep food fresh, but for a shorter period. Be sure to check a food's "best by" date on the label before buying or feeding it to your pet.

- Marketing terms such as "natural" or "premium" have no official legal or scientific definition. If you want to know what the manufacturer means by "human-grade ingredients" or "70 percent organic," or "quality," "natural," "premium," or "super premium," give the company a call and get some answers. Every can or bag of dog food must list contact information for the manufacturer on the label.

PRESCRIPTION DIETS

Several pet food companies make prescription diets for conditions such as liver or kidney disease, obesity, joint health, allergies, and for the senior dog. Veterinary food formulas often have natural preservatives such as vitamin E rather than chemical preservatives. We are fortunate to have these products available if our dogs are ever diagnosed with a problem.

THE VEGETARIAN DIET

Vegetarian dog food can provide your dog with a wide range of nutrients derived from vegetables, fruits, grains, and nuts. However, most veterinarians insist that meat should form a part of your dog's balanced diet. That doesn't mean that vegetables, fruits, and grains aren't good for your dog. It's just that dogs need protein. In nature, they are carnivorous scavengers. So even though dogs can survive on vegetarian food, that food would need to include a high level of protein from easily digestible sources, such as eggs and milk. Protein derived from meat

Once you know what to look for on the label, you can find dog food that provides your Shih Tzu with the best nutrition.

is of the highest quality and is the easiest for your dog to digest. Your dog can use more of the nutrients from meat protein than other kinds—you can see the difference in smaller, firmer stools.

However, protein alone doesn't make up a healthy dog diet. Complex carbohydrates give your dog energy. Dietary fiber maintains intestinal health. Vitamin A keeps eyes and skin healthy. Vitamin D keeps his bones and teeth strong. Vitamin E keeps his reproductive and intestinal systems healthy. Vitamin K is good for his blood. And B vitamins support almost all areas of your dog's health. Foods that provide these benefits are vegetables, especially carrots and green plants; fruits; some nuts (but not walnuts or macadamia nuts, which are toxic to dogs); and grains including brown rice and corn.

Vegetarian dog treats are an excellent way to provide snacks that are nutritious for your dog, regardless of his diet.

> **BE AWARE!**
> Some foods can cause serious health problems for your Shih Tzu. These include chocolate, caffeine, onions, avocado pits, raisins, grapes, macadamia nuts, mushrooms, raw eggs, and the artificial sweetener Xylitol, which can cause low blood sugar and liver failure.

THE RAW OR BARF DIET

In recent years, feeding dogs raw meat has become increasingly popular. This has sparked health concerns because of the risk of foodborne illnesses in pets as well as the public health risks of zoonotic infections (those transferred from animal to man).

Proponents of the raw meat diet say it improves dogs' performance, coat, body odor, teeth, and breath. While high-performance dogs, such as racing Greyhounds and sled dogs, have been fed raw meat diets for years, the trend to feed raw meat to companion dogs is recent.

One problem with the raw diet is the possibility of the presence of *Escherichia coli*, *Salmonella*, and *Campylobacter* in the raw meat. Bacteria are not the only health concern; there are also parasites and protozoal organisms that can be transmitted in raw meat, even meat labeled fit for human consumption. Studies have shown that animals fed raw protein diets shed significantly higher amounts of pathogenic bacteria in their stool than those fed cooked proteins. Indications are that this may put some people at risk, as compared to pets being fed commercially prepared or cooked home-made diets.

The most popular raw diet is BARF (Biologically Appropriate Raw Food), formulated by Dr. Ian Billinghurst and Robert Mueller, who together have more than 50 years of combined study in raw foods. A "biologically appropriate" diet for a dog is one consisting of raw whole foods similar to those eaten by dogs' wild ancestors. The food must contain muscle meat, bone, fat, organ meats, and vegetable and fruit materials. Proponents of the diet claim it maximizes health, longevity, and reduces allergies and vet bills. The diet is based on human-grade whole foods including raw meat, finely ground bones, offal, and other healthy ingredients such as fruit and vegetables. The diet can be prepared at home or is commercially available.

Feeding any raw diet is a decision only you can make, but if you go this route your dog's vet should be informed.

THE HOME-COOKED DIET

Some people like to cook for their dogs, even if they don't cook for their spouse! A homemade diet consists of 40 percent meat, 30 percent vegetables, and 30 percent starch, which often consists of oatmeal, pasta, rice, or potatoes. If you decide to go the homemade route, be sure to share your diet plan with your veterinarian or a canine nutritionist to make sure it meets the minimum daily requirements.

A home-cooked diet should not be confused with just giving your dog table scraps. In fact, it is best for your dog and best for you not to feed him from the table. This not only can lead to obesity but also can become very annoying, especially when you have guests. If you do give him scraps in his bowl, make sure they are only as good as what you would eat—for example, no bones and no fat, which could cause pancreatitis.

HOW MUCH SHOULD YOU FEED YOUR SHIH TZU?

Puppies should be fed a high-quality, age-appropriate food three or four times a

Most vets recommend meat as a major part of your dog's diet, but vegetables like carrots can be part of an overall healthy diet.

day, and should be allowed to eat all they want. A puppy needs about twice as many calories per pound (kg) as an adult, and puppies' little tummies can hold only so much at a time. Snacks are fine, but they can amount to a big part of the puppy's total intake, so keep the snacks small and nutritious.

PUPPY POINTER

Adhering strictly to a feeding schedule for your puppy will aid in housetraining. He will learn to relieve himself right after mealtime and acquire good habits early.

Once your dog becomes an adult, measure his food and feed him once or twice a day. (Note: You can begin giving your Shih Tzu adult food at around nine to ten months of age when he is close to achieving his adult weight.) Reduce the amount recommended on the label by 25 percent to prevent overeating, then make adjustments based on your dog's health and weight. You can mix some canned food along with the dry to make it more palatable. To prevent finicky eating, take away whatever's left in his bowl if he hasn't finished it in 20 minutes. And give him plenty of exercise to keep him fit.

Be sure to count those dog treats in his total intake of food. Healthy snacks such as fruits and vegetables can help curb obesity and give your dog some extra nutrients. Apple slices, carrot sticks, banana slices, and frozen vegetables, especially green beans, are canine favorites.

IS YOUR DOG THE PROPER WEIGHT?

If you're unsure as to whether your Shih Tzu is overweight, use the Body Condition Scoring (BCS) system. It is easy to do.

- First, check the ribs by putting your hands on the dog's sides, over the ribs. Rub over the ribs gently. There are 13 on each side. If you cannot feel or count at least three or four ribs, your dog is probably overweight.
- Next, look at the dog from the side. The abdomen should be tucked up in front of the back legs. Now look from the top. You should see a definite waist behind the dog's ribs.

The BSC system rates dogs from "Emaciated," where all ribs and lumbar vertebrae along the spine are visible from a distance and the dog has lost body fat and muscle, to "Morbid," where there are massive deposits of fat in most areas and the abdomen is obviously protruding. The goal for the dog owner is "Ideal," where the "ribs can be felt without an excess of fat covering them; there is a thin layer of fat over them. The waist can be observed behind the ribs when viewed from above. Abdomen is tucked up when viewed from the side."

Each change in BCS score is associated with about 11 percent change in the dog's body weight. This varies by breed, of course. In a smaller dog like the Shih Tzu, each category represents a larger percentile change in body weight.

DEALING WITH OBESITY

If your dog is just a little overweight, you can start him on an exercise and reduced calorie food program. If he is severely overweight, it might be better to have your vet assist you in his regimen.

Cut out table scraps, if applicable. Cut down on treats no matter how cute your Shih Tzu looks posing at the cookie jar. If your 15-pound (7 kg) dog has a 500 to 700 calorie allowance per day, just one or two treats can make up one-third of the calorie allotment for the day.

New low-calorie foods are coming out all the time for dogs. Try a mix of the new food with what you are using now until he is eating all diet food. Some are more palatable than others, so you may have to experiment. Or you can simply cut back on what you are feeding, as long as your dog doesn't become a pesky beggar. Keep a daily treat checklist so family members don't give multiple treats.

The average Shih Tzu does not need a lot of exercise, but a daily walk on his leash or a play date in the back yard is always appreciated. If he is starting to put on a few pounds, increase his activity level. Don't make him do too much at first. If he seems to be getting tired, stop for the day. You can increase the time period a little as you go along.

Ignore those begging eyes—it doesn't take long for too many snacks to make your Shih Tzu overweight.

It is a myth that dogs gain weight after being neutered or spayed. Just like humans, dogs gain weight if they eat too much and exercise too little or if they are genetically programmed to be overweight. The weight gain you may notice is most likely caused by continuing to feed a high-energy diet to a dog who is reducing his need for energy as he reaches adult size.

FEEDING THE SENIOR DOG

Just as a human's metabolic rate slows down as we age, so does a dog's. After the age of nine or ten your Shih Tzu is regarded as a senior. Since small breeds live longer, they seem to age more slowly and remain active longer. Once they become less active, senior dogs will require fewer calories in order to prevent obesity. If in good health, your senior will have similar nutritional needs as an adult, but with fewer fats and more protein and fiber to aid in digestion. Some older dogs tend to gain weight even when they eat fewer calories. Commercial foods for less active, obese, and senior dogs may be your best bet to feed during those twilight years.

Some senior dogs lose a great deal of weight even if their health is good. Mild loss of muscle mass, especially in the hind legs, may be seen with old age. This is a normal part of the aging process and is to be expected. As long as the dog is otherwise healthy, you can supplement his diet with cottage cheese; lean, drained ground beef; and maybe a weight-gain dog food if there is one that suits his needs. If the weight loss is accompanied by muscle weakness, falling, or any other unusual symptoms, consult your veterinarian to rule out any disease processes going on.

Some things to avoid in the senior dog's diet are excessive carbohydrates; food and treats high in sugar; bad fat sources such as animal-meal or animal by-products; table scraps and treats made for humans; highly processed foods; treats made with preservatives and fillers; and foods with reduced levels of protein.

As dogs age, they may have a reduced ability to absorb nutrients. This can lead to dry, brittle coats, thickened skin, and susceptibility to skin infections. Too much fat can cause acute or chronic pancreatitis, especially in spayed females.

Extra pounds on an older pet may contribute to joint disease, congestive heart failure, and diabetes. Exercise is a vital part of preventing weight gain, but be sure to limit the intensity of your dog's workouts and follow a normal routine. Gear the activity toward your dog's fitness level and health condition.

WHAT ABOUT SUPPLEMENTS?

Reputable commercial dog foods have more than enough protein, fat, vitamins, and minerals to keep your dog healthy. In fact, *too many* minerals for puppies can lead to severe skeletal problems as they grow. If there seems to be a problem with your Shih Tzu, contact your vet first.

Consult with your Shih Tzu's veterinarian before giving your dog any supplements.

FATTY ACIDS

One thing Shih Tzu owners may notice is a sparse or brittle coat or dry skin. This could be the sign of low thyroid, Cushing's disease, or allergies, or he could simply need a supplement of omega-3 fatty acids for coat health.

Omega-3 fatty acids have been suggested for a number of health issues in humans and in dogs. They are beneficial for coat and skin health, and recent studies on the effects of omega-3 fatty acids (fish oil) for the treatment of osteoarthritis in dogs have shown an improved ability to rise from a resting position, play, and bear weight on the affected limbs. No significant adverse side effects from the fish oil supplementation have been reported. Arthritis is estimated to affect up to 20 percent of dogs over one year of age. The effectiveness of fish oil varies from dog to dog.

GLUCOSAMINE/CHONDROITIN

A popular supplement taken by humans and their dogs is glucosamine and chondroitin, which are excellent for maintaining joint health. Glucosamine dog supplements have been shown to improve and prevent the symptoms of joint pain in dogs. Unless there is a medical reason to suggest otherwise, this should be given at the first sign of joint pain.

ANTIOXIDANTS

Antioxidants help protect your dog from infection, keep him alert, and let him live a longer, healthier life. Selenium acts as an antioxidant in your dog's body; green tea extract, alpha lipolic acid, and Siberian ginseng are some other natural dog supplements that have antioxidant properties.

CONSULT YOUR VET

Whatever supplement you choose, make sure it is intended for dogs and that it suits your Shih Tzu's age and size. If you're choosing a supplement to treat a medical condition, especially a systemic disease, consult your veterinarian first. Your vet may prescribe a specialized vitamin supplement for the treatment of a medical condition.

GROOMING
YOUR SHIH TZU

Grooming a Shih Tzu is time intensive but can be a pleasurable experience for both you and your dog. But it also can be a power struggle if he is not trained to lie down quietly while you brush and trim him. The amount of grooming necessary is something you need to consider when choosing this breed as your companion.

Often a professional groomer is the best option, but there are things you can do in between visits to cut down on the time, stress, and cost of using a groomer.

Your Shih Tzu breeder may have started training your puppy to lie on his side from an early age. This makes it easier for you to brush and trim him throughout his life. Continue this training from his first day home, even if he does not have enough hair to brush. Brushing stimulates blood circulation, and for this reason it can be relaxing for your dog. It also stimulates natural oils and gets rid of loose hair, preventing little tumbleweeds of dead hair floating around your house.

HEALTH CHECK

A grooming session is also a good way to give your Shih Tzu a health check.
- Check for skin irritation, fleas, ticks, lumps, or anything else out of the ordinary. Dry, dull skin and brittle hair can be a sign of systemic disease or simply a need for a supplement or change in food.
- Check the eyes for discharge. Shih Tzu do produce tears that can cause clumping at the corner of the eye, and this needs to be wiped away. If the discharge seems like too much, it may be the result of a medical issue such as dry eye, allergies, or infection.
- Check the teeth for signs of tartar buildup or gum disease. If your dog has "doggy" breath, he probably needs his teeth cleaned, or it may indicate a more serious problem affecting body systems such as the liver or kidneys.
- Check the ears for signs of redness or swelling. Ear mites and infections require medical treatment. Your vet may need to treat the ears and prescribe medication.

GROOMING EQUIPMENT

Today's grooming equipment has gone far beyond the brush and comb. You can find dog mouthwash, the electric toothbrush, ionizing brushes, aromatherapy shampoos and cologne, bathrobes—you name it. If you can buy it for humans, you can buy it for your dog.

If you decide to try your hand at grooming your own Shih Tzu, here are some items you should have.
- Good-quality cushion-based steel pin brush

- Greyhound comb or other metal comb with both wide and narrowly spaced teeth
- Flea comb or small cat comb for around the eyes
- Hair clips large enough to grasp a thick lock of hair
- Nail clippers, which come in the guillotine type, the pliers style, or cat nail clippers; some people prefer the nail grinder, but you have to be careful not to catch errant hairs in the grinder while using.
- Good-quality trimming scissors
- Small round-tipped scissors
- Styptic stick or powder in case of a bleeding nail
- Cornstarch to keep the face dry
- Spray bottle
- Shampoo and conditioner made for a coated breed or a human hair product
- Baby shampoo or foam wash for around the eyes
- Detangling spray
- Ear powder and cleaner
- Toothbrush and toothpaste made for dogs
- Latex bands (the type used by orthodontists) for the topknot
- Bows
- A tack box or other container for all of the supplies

Whether your Shih Tzu is kept in a long, flowing coat (left) or a shorter puppy cut (right), you'll still have to brush him several times a week.

You may want to invest in a professional fold-up grooming table to give you a non-slip grooming surface. These tables have ridges that prevent your dog's feet from slipping. Be sure never to leave him on the table unattended.

You can set up the table in your den and brush your Shih Tzu at your leisure while watching television. A lot of breeders and exhibitors do the very same thing!

BRUSHING YOUR SHIH TZU

There is a lot of work involved for your Shih Tzu to have that "luxurious, double-coated, dense, long, and flowing coat," beginning with preventing mats.

In order to prevent matting and to keep your dog in a regular routine, you should brush him several times per week. You may find out as you go along that you can get by with once a week —it depends on the length, texture, and thickness of the coat. Some coats are silkier, some are coarser, others are in between. Having your Shih Tzu clipped in a short cut will not save you from brushing. The shorter clips mat just as fast as the long coats, sometimes even faster. However, they are easier and less time-consuming to keep brushed out and bathed.

THE BRUSHING ROUTINE

Grooming will be much easier if you take the time to train your Shih Tzu to lie on his side, stand quietly on a non-skid surface, or lie on his back on your lap. Using the hair clips, section off several top layers of coat so you have access to

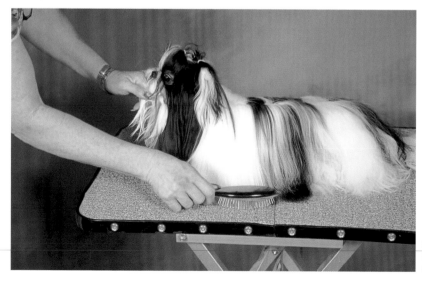

Use a pin brush for brushing the under and outer coat layers.

the undercoat. Using the pin brush, brush the under layer first, and then brush the coat layer by layer until each section is finished. Using the spray bottle, lightly mist the coat to prevent static. The spray bottle can contain tap water, water mixed with a bit of conditioner, or an anti-static conditioner. You may prefer to brush the coat with your brush dipped in cornstarch to catch dirt and oil.

Brush from the skin to beyond the end of the hair to prevent breakage. When you get to the legs, ears, and around the face, you will need to switch to a smaller brush or comb. Have the dog stand or sit as necessary.

If you find a mat—and you will—sprinkle it with cornstarch or spray it, depending on which method you are using. Try to separate it with your fingers or try the end tooth of the comb. Separating a mat is an art, and you will soon be a pro if you are patient and figure out which grooming tool works best for you. As tempting as it is to just cut out the mat, keep in mind where it is and how it will look once your dog is all groomed and bathed.

Long-coated breeds like the Shih Tzu tend to mat under the legs and around the ears. These are also the most difficult places to work. The ears are very sensitive, so you have to be careful not to injure the tissue with the teeth of the comb.

For a shorter coat, you still need to prevent mats. Use the same grooming tools, including the cornstarch, and brush from the skin out. It is easier to work out the mats in a short coat, but sometimes they form even faster, especially when the dog plays and rolls on the carpet, causing static.

BATHING YOUR SHIH TZU

There are two important things to remember when bathing your Shih Tzu.
1.	Make sure all of the mats have been brushed out and the ears, eyes, and feet have been groomed.
2.	The key to bathing your dog is to bathe him just before he needs it.

Okay, the first point is obvious. But how do you know "before he needs" his bath? You will know, eventually. It will become instinctive. When the coat starts getting dirty you will see that it is more likely to clump. That is too late! You'll need to act when your dog barely starts to feel dirty.

Unlike dogs with fur, Shih Tzu have hair that needs a shampoo and conditioner made for coated breeds or one made for human hair—that is, not too alkaline.

Since not all will have the same coat type, you may have to try several products to find the best one for your dog. It is all trial and error, but once you find the right formula, you will be set.

Pollutants, humidity, and dry air can all change the consistency of the coat, just as with your hair. Shampoos formulated with aloe vera, tea tree oil, fatty acids, and other ingredients help skin and coat recover.

Wrap your Shih Tzu in a towel before you get ready to blow dry the coat.

THE BATHING ROUTINE

When it is time for the bath, place a non-skid mat in the bottom of the sink or tub. Saturate the coat with warm water, preferably with a spray hose, and apply the shampoo. Treat the coat as if it were an angora sweater. The gentler you are with the coat, the fewer tangles you will have later. Use baby shampoo or foam for around the eyes to prevent irritation.

Rinse the coat thoroughly and apply conditioner. Let the conditioner saturate the coat for a few minutes for optimum benefit. Rinse. Bundle up your dog in a thick towel and get ready to dry.

Lay the dog on his side. Using your hair clips, pin up the outer layers of the coat and dry the undercoat first, brushing it the entire time to keep it straight.

The best type of dryer comes on a stand, leaving your hands free. Some stand dryers sit on the floor, others on the table. Stand dryers made specifically for pets are best because the heat temperature is milder than a human hair dryer. Even so, you'll still want to keep tabs on how warm your dog's skin gets, as you don't want dryer burn.

Dry the hair layer by layer until it is all dry. Even when you think it is dry enough—dry it more. This is one of the keys to preventing mats. You can use the end of your comb or a knitting needle to make a straight part down the back.

Drying the short coat will not take as long, but the same principles still apply. You still need to check for mats as you brush, and the coat must be completely dry to prevent future matting.

Once your dog is thoroughly dry, and if the hair is long enough, trim the feet and coat. Cut any straggly long hairs and tidy up the feet. Trim gradually—you can always take more off, but you can't put it back on!

Most Shih Tzu coats are very forgiving and will survive a few mistakes on your part. Just relax and enjoy the benefits of your hard work. It will get easier.

THE TOPKNOT

The hair on the Shih Tzu's head should be pulled into a topknot. The show-style topknot is an art form for those who are in the sport of exhibiting Shih Tzu. It involves curling irons, special gels, and lots of poofs! Most people learn from a mentor in the breed who is also sharing knowledge of grooming, exhibiting, breeding, and so on. If you would like to see how this fashionable yet complicated topknot is achieved, visit the Shih Tzu Club of America (STCA) website at www.americanshihtzuclub.org/show_knots.

For outside the show ring, a more casual-style topknot can look very cute. The easiest way to do a casual topknot is to simply bundle the hair on top of the head with one or two latex bands (like the type orthodontists use for braces), add a bow, and be done. This looks especially cute with a short clip (if you've left enough hair on the head to bundle). Practice will make perfect. The most important thing is to not tie the bands too tight, causing the hair to pull around the eyes.

If you want a slightly more advanced casual style, you can try this technique.

The easiest way to do a topknot is to simply bundle the hair on top of the head with one or two latex bands and add a bow.

You'll need small latex bands and a parting comb to make it easy to grasp sections of the hair. You will be making two topknots, one in front and one in back, then joining them.

- For the front topknot, part the hair from the outside corner of each eye and hold it up, making an inverted V.
- Make another part across the skull from ear to ear, about in the middle.
- Make sure the ear hair is brushed down and doesn't get tangled in the hair you are grasping.
- Gather the hair with a latex band, making a nice poof on the underside of the band, and leaving the hair loose on top of the band.
- For the back topknot, make a half-moon part at the back of the head and bring that section of hair forward and band it.
- Put a bow on the front section.
- Join the two sections together with one or two bands and spread the hair out in a nice pattern on top.

It takes practice, and you can even experiment with your own way to do it. You may even want to try two separate topknots, side by side.

Topknots can tangle quickly, so you may want to redo them at least every few days for easier maintenance. That way you catch mats before they become a chore.

EAR CARE

Dogs like Shih Tzu with drop-down ears are especially susceptible to infections. Check your Shih Tzu's ears—they should be clean and pink. If you see a brown or black ear discharge it could be ear mites, which can cause intense irritation of the ear canal. Mites can cause head shaking and scratching of the ears. Redness or swelling could be caused by a yeast or bacterial infection. All of these conditions require medical treatment. Your vet may need to treat the ears and prescribe medication.

If the inside of the ear has a lot of hair, it may increase the chance of an ear infection. To help prevent this:
- Sprinkle the inside of the ear with ear powder.
- Give the powder a minute or two to numb the area, then grasp a small amount

of hair and pull it out.
- Repeat until the hair is gone.

Many people leave ear cleaning to a groomer or vet, since your dog may not be happy at all with this procedure. Never use cotton tip applicators in the ear canal. A cotton puff is much safer.

EYE CARE

Grooming around the eyes helps prevent eye infections and other medical problems. If your dog's eye is bloodshot, cloudy, or partially closed, consult your vet at once. The Shih Tzu's eyes are large and round, and occasionally prominent. Be careful with any instruments around the eye that could cause damage.

To keep your Shih Tzu's eyes healthy:
- Use cornstarch or a baby washcloth to keep the area around the eyes dry.
- Using your flea comb or cat comb, carefully remove any debris from the corner of the eye and from the eye lashes.
- Use commercial eye stain products formulated for dogs, making sure the ingredients are safe.
- Make sure there are no short hairs that irritate the eye.
- If you choose to clip the hair away from the eyes, use round-tipped scissors and be very, very careful! Hold the scissors at the inside corner of the eye at a 45 degree angle with the scissor tips facing up and beyond the eye. Clip

Sometimes a teething Shih Tzu puppy will get eye stains.

the hair as closely as you can without touching any tissue. Repeat on the other side. Some people use small clippers, like mustache clippers, but again, be careful.

Often a Shih Tzu will get eye stains, especially when teething. This pinkish pigment is due to oxidation of elements in the tears, much like rusting metal. Ask

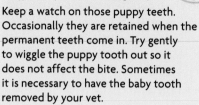

your vet about using tetracycline powder orally as an antioxidant. Because this drug is rarely used for dogs anymore, and you will not be using it at a therapeutic dosage, it won't matter if the dog builds up immunity to it. It is unlikely tetracycline will ever be prescribed for any type of infection. Puppies usually outgrow eye stains as they get older. Do not use tetracycline in a dog whose adult teeth have not yet grown in—it can cause discoloration!

Hard water can contribute to staining around the eyes and mouth, as well as food or treats with certain dyes, especially red dye.

DENTAL CARE

Small dogs have small mouths. Crowded teeth cause more plaque and tartar buildup and, eventually, tooth loss. Gum infection can lead to systemic disease by spilling bacteria into the bloodstream, leading to the heart, liver, kidneys, and brain, causing damage to those organs.

If periodontal disease develops, the gums will eventually recede, causing tooth and bone loss, bleeding, and pain. Canine dentistry has evolved at about the same pace as human dentistry, so you can take your dog for periodontal surgery, orthodontics, root canals, caps, etc. However, it is painful for your dog and is very expensive. This is why it's so important to incorporate teeth brushing into the grooming routine.

BRUSHING YOUR SHIH TZU'S TEETH

Brush your dog's teeth as often as possible but at least once a week with a toothpaste designed for dogs, formulated not to foam. Try to brush the inner surfaces as well as the outer, and get the crevice where the tooth and gum meet. If a toothbrush does not work well for you, try dental pads, gauze, or sponges. They are not quite as effective, but will help keep the teeth and gums clean.

Tooth scalers, like the ones your dentist uses, are not recommended for your Shih Tzu. You can easily tear the gum, allowing for infection or for bacteria to enter the bloodstream. Additives for your dog's drinking water may help with tartar control, although some work better than others. You can also give your dog breath tablets that can help with doggie breath.

In addition to brushing, give your dog dry kibble and hard biscuits designed for tartar control. There are also dental chews and toys with knobby protrusions that are designed to keep teeth healthy. Raw vegetables are also a good choice.

Sometimes genetics will play a role in your Shih Tzu's dental health, even with the most meticulous brushing regimen. In this case, a professional teeth cleaning is necessary, which we'll discuss further in Chapter 6.

NAIL CARE

One of the cutest things about a Shih Tzu is his big fuzzy feet, especially when he paws at you for a treat. That fuzzy foot requires some care, not only cosmetic but also health-wise.

A dog's nails need to be trimmed on a regular basis. If they become too long they can actually interfere with his walking. Untrimmed nails can even split, resulting in pain and bleeding, or curl under and grow into the pad.

Get your Shih Tzu used to nail trimming at an early age.

TRIMMING YOUR SHIH TZU'S NAILS

Each nail has a blood vessel, called the quick, running through the center. The quick contains sensitive nerve endings that, when accidentally clipped, cause pain and bleeding. The prospect of snipping a dog's toenails and causing bleeding is daunting to many pet owners. Proper technique can reduce this possibility, but even the most seasoned groomer can clip a nail too short. If this happens, use a styptic pencil or powder to stop the bleeding. In spite of the blood, it is not as bad as you think. The pain does not last long. Sometimes it is worse for the owner than the dog.

BE AWARE!
In addition to keeping your Shih Tzu's nails trimmed, be sure to trim the hair from between his pads to prevent matting that could hurt his paws. Small round-ended scissors are best for this task.

Clip the nails with your dog on his side, standing, or even in your lap—whatever works. Hold the paw in one hand and the trimmer in the other. Take a deep breath. The key is to clip the nail to within approximately 2 millimeters of the quick.

Shih Tzu can have light- or dark-colored nails, sometimes even both on the same dog. Light-colored nails are easier to trim because you can see the blood vessels and nerves. Trim dark-colored nails in several small layers to reduce the chance of cutting into the quick. As you cut the nail deeper, you will see a gray to pink oval starting to appear at the top of the cut surface of the nail. Stop trimming at this point, as additional trimming will cut into the quick. You can file the end of the nail to smooth the surface.

Some Shih Tzu have dewclaws with nails on the front legs or (rarely) on the back legs. Many breeders opt to have the dewclaws removed shortly after birth to prevent them from catching on things or ripping off in play. If your dog has dewclaws, those nails have to be clipped as well.

While you are training your dog to lie on his side for brushing, get him accustomed to having his feet handled. Many dogs absolutely hate this part of grooming, even before they hear the first clip of the blades. Make your dog feel secure and praise him every time he lets you finish a foot. Bear in mind that even the best-mannered dog is capable of biting when in distress.

PADS

Keep the hair between the pads cleaned out to prevent mats that cause pain when walking. Small round-ended scissors are best for this task. First, hold the scissors parallel to the foot and trim the excess hair. Then, while holding the dog

A well-trained dog will make trimming your Shih Tzu much easier for both of you.

very still, separate the pads and carefully trim out that hair. Be careful! You don't want to nick the delicate skin.

Be on the lookout for cysts forming between the pads. They can be quite painful and will need to be removed surgically and the area treated with antibiotics. Cysts are infections in the sebaceous (oil) glands or the follicles. Watch for any early signs of redness, swelling, or lesions between the toes.

Check the pads for drying or cracking. Cocoa butter or shea butter products can help ease this problem. The pads of the feet act as a shock absorber for the foot and leg and contain eccrine (sweat) glands that allow a dog to lose heat, or sweat, through his paws.

THE "OTHER END"

It is beneficial to keep the area under the tail around the anus clipped to prevent debris from attaching. You may also want to trim around the dog's private areas to keep them cleaner.

You may see your dog scoot his rear across the floor at some point. Usually this is caused by two tiny scent glands on each side of the anus. These anal glands enable the dog to mark his territory and identify other dogs. They are normally emptied when the dog defecates. Occasionally they will become too full or even impacted or infected, and have to be emptied manually. This is an unpleasant task best left to your groomer or vet.

FINDING A PROFESSIONAL GROOMER

If you decide to have your Shih Tzu professionally groomed, ask for referrals in order to find someone who is not only talented but also treats his or her clients well. The grooming experience should be a positive one for your dog.

You and the groomer can decide how often your dog needs to be groomed. If you are good at keeping mats at bay, you can probably wait longer between visits. If you want to keep your dog in a short clip, the visits will be more frequent.

Referrals are often the best way to find a good groomer. There are no requirements for groomers to be licensed by a government agency, but many are certified or registered by a local or national association.

Certification may not even be an issue. If the groomer is kind to your dog and presents your dog with a look that pleases you, that may be all you need. It is important that the dog looks forward to his grooming sessions and comes home happy.

You may want to call ahead and check on prices based on your breed and the condition your dog is in. Be honest if the dog is matted. This will take more of the groomer's time and cost you more money.

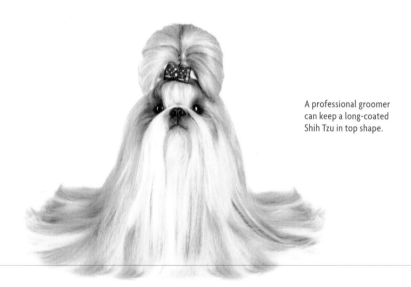

A professional groomer can keep a long-coated Shih Tzu in top shape.

My dog Libby is so happy to go for her "spa day" at the groomer I can barely get her leash on before she bolts to the car and jumps into her crate. When we get to the salon, I take off her leash so she can run down the hall to the grooming room. I can hear her groomers say, "Libby is here!" It's only because I found the right groomer that Libby has such a positive reaction to her grooming routine.

Make sure the grooming facility is clean and the grooming professionals are friendly and courteous, to you and to your dog. With a breed like a Shih Tzu, who has to be dried with a hair dryer, check to see what method is used. Do they use a stand-up or hand-held blow dryer, or a cage dryer where the dog is actually in an enclosed cage? Make sure the dogs are checked consistently if they use the latter method.

A grooming shop will probably ask for your dog's medical history, and may even require proof of a recent kennel cough vaccination. They will want to know the name of your vet in case there is a medical emergency. This is for your dog's protection and that of the other dogs and cats being groomed.

Ask whether the groomer ever uses sedation for an unruly dog. This may not be acceptable to you, or you may want the sedative prescribed by your vet. By the same token, let the groomer know of any particular requirements your dog may have, such as diabetes, epilepsy, or, arthritis so he or she can be aware of possible problems. And let the groomer know if your dog is a biter—it is only fair to everyone.

Finally, do not be afraid to tell the groomer exactly what you want. If you don't want your Shih Tzu trimmed like a Schnauzer, make that clear. Have realistic expectations, though. If your dog is matted, the groomer may not be able to save enough hair to present the look you want. It may take a few trips to get your Shih Tzu looking exactly like you want, but the effort will be worth it.

HEALTH OF YOUR SHIH TZU

Once your new Shih Tzu graces your home with his presence, his health is in your hands. Finding a good veterinarian and making yourself familiar with health issues should be a priority for the benefit of your new family member.

FINDING A VETERINARIAN

When choosing a vet, you should consider the same factors as you would in choosing any medical professional. Factors like location, office hours, payment options, and the range of medical services are all important considerations. Here are some suggestions from the American Veterinary Medical Association (AVMA) about what to look for:

• Who covers the practice when your doctor is unavailable?
• Is there an after-hours emergency clinic in your area?
• How do the staff and doctors interact with your pet?
• Does the hospital accept pet insurance policies?
• Does the vet have a network of specialists for referrals?
• Are the doctors members of a professional veterinary association?

Take time to select the clinic you feel can provide for your needs and the medical needs of your dog. After all, this will be a very important partnership during the life of your new companion.

THE FIRST VISIT

It's important to take your Shih Tzu puppy (or newly adopted dog) for an exam as soon as possible, definitely within a week of bringing him home, to make sure everything is all right. If the vet finds a serious problem, you will want to contact the breeder immediately to discuss your options. Certain illnesses might be covered under your contract. A reputable breeder will want to know about any problem with the dog and will stand behind the guarantee of a healthy puppy.

Your first visit to the vet with your new puppy should be a positive experience. Take along his favorite treats, a toy, or even a family member he is attached to. Take him into the clinic in his crate or carry-on bag to minimize exposure to germs. Let him

Finding the right vet is an important part of keeping your Shih Tzu healthy.

come out of the crate directly onto the exam room table if possible, and praise him.

As he learns some basic obedience, it will be easier to get him to behave during his examination. Praise him when he is good and give him a treat if it does not interfere with the exam. If you have a vet who is rough with your dog and makes him fearful, consider changing clinics. Going for medical procedures is a fact of life, and he should feel safe and you should not have to worry about his well-being unnecessarily.

PUPPY POINTER

Make it a practice to take your puppy to the park after each vet visit so he will have something to look forward to (after his shots, of course). Take him along with you to the vet clinic when you go to pick up medications or food so that he can just go in, hang out, and leave. The idea is to make going to the vet as positive an experience as you can for your Shih Tzu.

Talk to your vet about spay or neuter options for your puppy. Ask what types of preventive measures are recommended based on the health concerns in your community. Express any concerns you may have, whether financial or about a procedure. It is better that the vet understands your concerns in order to assist you with options.

THE ANNUAL EXAMINATION

A good way to remember the annual exam is to schedule it on your dog's birthday, or during his birthday month. This exam gives your vet an opportunity to discover any changes in your pet's health and catch him up on his vaccinations and other recurrent treatments.

In the waiting room, all dogs and cats should be restrained. Other dogs may be ill or aggressive, so you want to keep yours in your lap or take him in his carrier if that will make him feel more secure.

Make a list of questions so you won't forget what to ask, and take notes during the exam. Let your vet know of any subtle changes in your dog's appearance or behavior. Make note of your dog's weight so you can keep track of any weight loss or gain at home. Also, ask if the clinic has literature pertaining to treatments or any preventive care you will be administering.

Your vet will probably order routine blood tests that can detect a number of illnesses long before they become serious. In the Shih Tzu, the test could warn about liver or kidney problems that may not be evident based on your dog's general health.

A fecal exam will detect parasites and diseases affecting the intestines. It is always a good idea to take along a stool sample so the vet will not have to extract a sample from the dog (uncomfortable). The fecal exam will detect internal parasites such as hookworms, roundworms, and whipworms. Tapeworms are usually found by the owner near the dog's anus and the base of the tail. (They look like rice-like segments.) Tapeworms are most commonly transmitted by fleas. A heartworm test is essential. This parasite lives in the hearts of dogs and can be anywhere from 6 to 10 inches (15 to 25 cm) in length. Treatment is risky and expensive, so don't pass up this simple blood test.

Preventive care can save you money in the long run by keeping your dog healthier and less likely to develop illnesses that can become expensive to treat.

VACCINATIONS

A breeder should not let a puppy leave his or her care without at least an initial puppy vaccination. Newborn puppies receive antibodies through their mother's milk. However, after your puppy is weaned, he needs vaccinations to help his body form new antibodies against disease.

Not all dogs should be vaccinated with all vaccines—there are at least 14 available! For example, some areas may have a heavy incidence of Lyme disease, while others may have very few cases. Your vet will consider your dog's risks in order to customize a vaccination program. Let the vet know whether your dog

There are four core vaccinations your Shih Tzu needs for good health.

will have contact with other dogs (such as at kennels, obedience classes, or dog parks), since these factors will affect your dog's risk of exposure. Make sure your vet is aware of any previous adverse reactions to vaccines.

CORE VACCINATIONS

These are the four core vaccinations your puppy needs for good health.

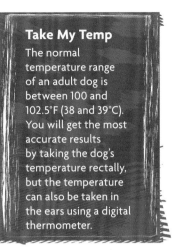

Take My Temp

The normal temperature range of an adult dog is between 100 and 102.5°F (38 and 39°C). You will get the most accurate results by taking the dog's temperature rectally, but the temperature can also be taken in the ears using a digital thermometer.

- *Parvovirus* is one of the most common infectious dog diseases in the United States. It is spread through contact with infected feces and can live on inanimate surfaces, making it virtually impossible to stop its spread. Parvovirus is deadly and treatment is costly.

- *Canine distemper* virus attacks the central nervous system, leading to seizures and death. Dogs can recover from distemper, but it can leave them with permanent brain damage.

- *Canine hepatitis*, if not treated quickly, can kill puppies in a matter of hours, before symptoms even manifest. If your dog recovers, he will be more vulnerable to kidney infections and may suffer serious permanent damage to his liver and eyesight.

- *Rabies vaccines* are required by law, and their frequency varies from state to state. Rabies in dogs causes aggressive behavior, seizures, and death. Rabies spreads through the saliva of the infected animal, and rabid animals are likely to attack.

  For many years it was considered necessary for dogs (and cats) to receive annual vaccinations. There is increasing evidence that immunity triggered by some vaccines provides protection beyond one year, while other vaccines may fail to protect for a full year. So a single vaccination schedule will not work well for all pets. Talk to your vet about what is right for your dog.

SIDE EFFECTS

Vaccines can occasionally cause side effects, but compared to the risk of *not* vaccinating, the risk is small. Here are some signs to watch out for:
- Pain, swelling, or redness at the injection site.
- A mild fever, decreased appetite, or depression.

- A mild cough if vaccinated with the intranasal bordetella and/or parainfluenza vaccine; the cough generally does not require treatment.

The most serious reaction to a vaccination is anaphylaxis. This is very rare—about one case occurs for every 15,000 doses administered—and usually occurs within minutes to hours (less than 24). It may cause shock, respiratory failure, or cardiac arrest, and can be fatal if not treated. Anaphylaxis can cause sudden diarrhea, vomiting, pale gums, cold limbs, fast heart rate, weak pulse, facial swelling, seizures and/or shock and possibly coma. The dog needs a shot of epinephrine immediately, followed by oxygen and IV fluids.

If you are concerned about the possibility of a vaccine reaction, have the shots given early in the morning so you can keep your eye on your dog throughout the day while the clinic is still open.

A puppy or a dog whose immune system is compromised or stressed in any way should not be vaccinated. He will not be able to develop the necessary immunities. Therefore, don't have your dog vaccinated while he is ill or on the day he is having a surgical procedure.

If you have a concern about a vaccination, antibody titers can measure whether your dog is protected from disease. They don't replace a vaccination program, but in some cases may help your vet determine whether your dog is protected.

SPAYING OR NEUTERING YOUR SHIH TZU

You should definitely consider spaying your female Shih Tzu or neutering your male. It's not only the ethical choice, it's also good for the health of your dog.

FEMALES

Most experts agree that females should be spayed before they have their first heat cycle, which can occur any time after the age six months. Spaying, or ovariohysterectomy, is the removal of both ovaries and the uterus.

Reasons to spay your female are:
- Estrogen is one of the primary causes of canine mammary cancer, the most common malignant tumor in dogs. The risk in dogs spayed prior to their first heat is 0.05 percent. It is 8 percent if spayed after one heat,

A breeder should not let a puppy leave her care without at least an initial puppy vaccination.

Spaying or neutering your Shih Tzu has many health benefits.

and 26 percent if spayed after the second heat.
- Tumors can occur in the uterus and ovaries.
- Some females experience false pregnancies resulting from hormonal fluctuations. A female's abdomen may be swollen, and she may make a nest; she may even adopt an object as a baby.
- Milk in the mammary glands can cause them to become infected.
- Females can develop pyometra (literally, pus in the uterus). Pyometra can be life-threatening, and an affected female will need to be spayed immediately. The surgery can be risky.
- There is always the risk of an unwanted pregnancy.
- There is no menopause in dogs. Unless spayed, females have heat cycles for their entire lives.
- There are also the sanitary aspects of a female in heat. Unless she is able to keep clean, there can be staining and odor associated with the cycle.

You may be thinking about breeding your female, but that is not a decision to be taken lightly. Consider the possibility that something could go wrong. She could have difficult labor, uterine or mammary gland infections, or even more serious concerns. Small dogs like the Shih Tzu occasionally need C-sections, which can be risky for her and add to the expense of the litter. After a C-section, the mother often has difficulty bonding with her babies, so that will be more work for you.

Also think very seriously about the problem of pet overpopulation. Maybe you feel you would have homes for the puppies from "that one litter" before you spay, but would those people do the responsible thing and have their puppies spayed or neutered? The cycle could go on and on if other owners are not responsible as well.

MALES

Neutering the male Shih Tzu is a much simpler matter. The procedure, in which both testicles are removed, is low risk and relatively inexpensive, especially for a small dog. There is some debate as to how early dogs can be neutered, but most dogs are neutered between five and eight months of age before unwanted behaviors have started. And a male dog doesn't care that he has been neutered—honestly!

Reasons to neuter your male are:

- Unneutered males can get testicular cancer.
- Unneutered males tend to mark their territory and want to roam.
- Unneutered males are more likely to be aggressive due to increased testosterone levels.
- Sexually active males can get sexually transmitted diseases such as brucellosis.
- There are fewer perianal hernias in older, neutered males; this condition requires costly surgery.
- Perianal adenomas (benign) or perianal adenocarcinomas (malignant) are very rare in neutered males.

Strangely enough, if you have your dog neutered he can have prosthetic testicles implanted. So, if you think your male dog is really going to have an identity crisis, consider that an option!

PARASITES

Shih Tzu owners may need to deal with fleas and ticks at some point in their dogs' lives.

FLEAS

Fleas are the bane of the dog owner's existence, not to mention a horrible nuisance to the dog. In one day, a single flea can bite your dog more than 400 times, consuming more than its body weight in blood. If left unchecked, a female flea can lay hundreds of eggs on your dog, perpetuating the cycle of flea infestation.

In some cases, flea bites can be dangerous. They can cause flea allergy dermatitis—an allergic reaction to proteins in flea saliva. This condition will require antihistamines, steroids, or even allergy shots to resolve. A pet's constant scratching can cause permanent hair loss and other skin problems. Even more disturbing, your dog can get a tapeworm if he ingests an infected flea. In dogs who are severely infested with fleas, or are chronically ill, the loss of blood from the flea bites can actually cause anemia and, in rare cases, death.

It is best to start preventive measures at the beginning of the flea season, which can vary depending on where you live. (September is the worst time for fleas in many climates.) There are hundreds of products available for prevention and treatment, ranging from oral medications that require a veterinarian's prescription to collars, sprays, dips, shampoos, and powders. Liquid products applied directly

Check your Shih Tzu for fleas and ticks after he's been outside.

to the pet's skin, often behind the neck, are highly effective. Some products kill only ticks or adult fleas—others break the flea life cycle by preventing flea eggs from developing into adult fleas.

Read the label carefully before use. A puppy, elderly dog, or one who has a chronic illness should not be treated without talking to your veterinarian. Once you have chosen a safe product (for your dog, not for the fleas!), follow directions exactly. After applying the product, wash your hands immediately with soap and water. If your pet shows symptoms of illness after treatment, call your veterinarian. Symptoms of a bad reaction may include poor appetite, depression, vomiting, diarrhea, or excessive salivation.

TICKS

Another parasitic nuisance is the tick. Tick bites can give your pet such infections as Lyme disease, ehrlichiosis (a bacterial infection), and Rocky Mountain spotted fever—and ticks can give those same infections to you. If you live in an area with severe tick infestation, you may want to consider giving your dog the vaccination for Lyme disease. Lyme disease is caused by a bacterium transmitted through the bite of the deer tick, also called the black-legged tick, which is no larger than the head of a pin.

If a tick is removed within 24 hours, the chances of its transmitting Lyme disease or other infections are greatly reduced. If you find a tick on your dog, use fine-point tweezers to grasp the tick as close to the skin as possible. Pull gently, and avoid squeezing the body of the tick. Clean the site of the bite, your hands, and the tweezers with disinfectant. You may want to wear protective gloves. You also may want to place the tick in a small container and take it to your vet for identification. Never use a burned match, petroleum jelly, or nail polish to try to remove ticks. Those methods are ineffective.

SHIH TZU IN SICKNESS AS WELL AS IN HEALTH

There are several breed-related health issues you should be aware of in the Shih Tzu.

BLADDER STONES

Bladder stones form when crystals in the urine aren't passed. These crystals bind together and form stones. Causes are heredity, untreated or frequent urinary tract infections, and certain medications. Symptoms include blood in the urine, painful urination, and licking the genital area. Treatment is using filtered water and dietary changes (such as a prescription diet available from your veterinarian). Surgery, referred to as cystotomy, is frequently necessary. The bladder is actually opened and the stones are removed and sent for analysis.

DENTAL PROBLEMS

As we mentioned in Chapter 5, because your Shih Tzu has a small mouth, his teeth are crowded together. This causes problems ranging from plaque and tartar buildup to tooth loss to infections that can cause organ damage.

Your veterinarian may recommend a professional teeth cleaning for you Shih Tzu. During a professional teeth cleaning, the vet will scale and polish the teeth and check for any disease processes. Often removal of a tooth is necessary if it is too damaged. A referral to a veterinary periodontist may be in order.

Antibiotics are often given before, during, and/or after a dental procedure to prevent bacteria from infecting the gums or leaking into the bloodstream. Dental procedures are almost always performed under anesthesia. Shih Tzu, with their short muzzles and noses, may have a narrow trachea (windpipe), requiring extra effort to move air through the airways. Ask your vet about using a gas anesthetic such as Isoflurane rather than general anesthesia to reduce risk.

EYE PROBLEMS

Brachycephalic dogs have shortened noses and very prominent eyes due to shallow orbits. Occasionally this causes lagophthalmos, an inability to properly close the eyelid over the cornea. This can lead to two serious problems for the Shih Tzu.

Exposure Keratitis

Exposure keratitis, or inflammation of the cornea, can range from benign to extremely serious. Chronic irritation can cause excessive pigmentation from deposits of melanin to the point of blindness. In its most severe form, a deep ulcer can cause the cornea to rupture. Diagnosis is made by examination with a magnification loupe and a focal beam of light. Once diagnosed, it is vital to remove the cause of irritation immediately. If the pigmentation has already caused vision loss, it sometimes can be lessened with superficial radiation or topical steroids.

Proptosis

Proptosis is where the eyelids clamp behind the eyeball itself and cause the venous blood from the eye not to be able to return. This causes a lack of oxygen to the retina and can lead to blindness within minutes. If a Shih Tzu has a proptosed globe it is an emergency! Veterinary care has to be sought immediately (within 20 minutes) in order to attempt to save vision and save the eye. Until you get to your vet, keep the eye moist with wet cotton and avoid any additional trauma.

Other Eye Problems

Other eye problems to be aware of are:

- Hereditary cataracts or juvenile cataracts can affect one or both eyes and may involve the lens partially or completely.
- Progressive retinal atrophy (PRA) is a degenerative disease of the retinal visual cells that progresses to blindness. It does not cause any pain to the dog.

Shih Tzu have very prominent eyes, which can lead to some eye problems.

- Distichiasis (a double row of eyelashes) and ectopic cilia are caused by irritation from the lashes, which are abnormally located at the eyelid margin. Both can cause severe scarring of the cornea and/or ulcers that could lead to blindness.
- Dry eye, or keratoconjunctivitis sicca, is due to decreased tear production and can make the cornea prone to damage, even ulceration.

Some of these problems can be prevented or minimized by keeping bits of hair and debris out of your dog's eyes. If you keep your Shih Tzu trimmed short, make sure there are no short hairs poking at his eyes or continually rubbing against them. This can alleviate some serious eye problems in the future.

JUVENILE RENAL DYSPLASIA

Juvenile renal dysplasia (JRD) is a developmental or genetic defect of the kidneys. It is found most commonly in Shih Tzu, Lhasa Apsos, and a few other breeds.

The affected puppy is born with relatively immature kidneys. In puppies older than eight weeks, there is excessive thirst and excessive volumes of urine, which is pale since the kidneys are no longer able to concentrate urine. Normal Shih Tzu puppies drink approximately one ounce (30 ml) of water per pound (.5 kg) of body weight daily when eight to ten weeks of age, but dogs with severe renal dysplasia may drink five times that quantity. Severely affected dogs have reduced body weight and will fail to thrive at two or three months of age and progress to renal failure quickly.

Many dogs are only slightly affected. They show no clinical signs, and the disease may not be detected by routine laboratory tests. The only way to detect JRD is by a kidney wedge biopsy, a major surgical procedure that is too risky to be used for diagnostic purposes.

Dogs with kidney failure don't show signs of uremia (waste products in the blood) until 75 percent of functioning kidney tissue is destroyed. Signs include apathy and depression, loss of appetite and weight, and an ammonia-like odor to the breath.

Visit the ASTC's website for information about the genetic test for juvenile renal dysplasia.

Treatment

Palliative treatment can extend the dog's life for months, or longer. This includes dietary modification, supplements, and subcutaneous (sub-Q) fluids given at home. The vitamin D hormone calcitriol, which has to be ordered through a compounding pharmacy, can be used to address problems with hyperparathyroidism that occur in renal failure. This hormone may also help patients with renal failure feel better.

Through funding by the American Shih Tzu Club (ASTC) and the American Lhasa Apso Club (ALAC), in 2006 Dr. Mary Whitley of Dogenes, Inc., discovered mutations on a gene associated with kidney development that appeared to be responsible for JRD, and developed genetic tests for them. The ASTC has an in-depth explanation of JRD and the genetic test on its web site (www.americanshihtzuclub.org).

LIVER SHUNT

Liver shunt, or portosystemic vascular anomaly (PSVA), can occur in the Shih Tzu and other small breeds. Often a condition known as microvascular dysplasia (MVD) occurs simultaneously. In dogs with PSVA, the accumulation of toxic material can cause neurological problems and even death, whereas MVD is usually clinically silent.

A liver shunt is a blood vessel that carries blood around the liver instead of through it. As a result, the liver cannot cleanse the blood or add important nutrients needed by the body and the brain. In some dogs, a liver shunt is a birth defect (congenital), while in others, multiple small shunts (acquired) form because of severe liver disease such as cirrhosis. Small breeds are more likely to develop shunts outside the liver, which are easier to correct surgically. Large breeds are more likely to develop shunts inside the liver.

In MVD, multiple tiny portal veins can be found inside the liver, causing microscopic shunting, but no illness. MVD is common and may also occur without PSVA.

You will usually see signs of a liver shunt before the dog is one year of age. Symptoms are poor growth, lethargy, excessive thirst and urination, diarrhea or vomiting, seizures, and behavioral changes such as confusion, circling, and head pressing. However, some dogs with PSVA and most dogs with MVD show no signs. The disease is detected when the vet measures serum bile acid concentration during treatment for an unrelated illness, or even during pre-anesthesia testing.

Serum bile acid testing is the best test, since dogs with PSVA or MVD are unable to clear bile acids from their circulation. Diagnosis with ultrasound is difficult and requires special expertise. Liver biopsy, a portogram (x-ray of the blood vessels to the liver), or scintigraphy (nuclear scan) are other options.

Treatment

Because many of the toxins produced in the intestines come from protein, it's important to reduce the amount of protein in the diet. Dogs with shunts need high-quality proteins made from milk or vegetables and are restricted to a protein content of 18 percent or less (on a dry matter basis). Pharmaceutical options to consider are:

- Neomycin is used orally to decrease the population of some types of bacteria in the intestine that may intensify the signs of liver disease.
- Denosyl has been shown to protect liver cells from cell death and may be useful in cell repair and healing.
- Lactulose changes the pH in the large intestines, which decreases absorption of ammonia and other toxins.

If you have a dog with a compromised liver, discuss with your vet the use of any drug that is processed through the liver—steroids, vaccines, heart worm or flea preventive, etc. These can be toxic to the liver.

Dogs who tend to do well with long-term medical management are usually older at the time of diagnosis and have more normal blood work and fewer severe clinical signs. Most improve immediately with proper diet, and about one-third of dogs treated medically will live a relatively long life.

Dogs diagnosed with liver shunt need a reduced-protein diet.

Researchers at Cornell University College of Veterinary Medicine are working to identify the genetic mutations responsible for PSVA/MVD. The goal is to discover a genetic test that would identify carriers. Among the breeds involved in the study is the Shih Tzu.

PANCREATITIS

Acute pancreatitis is inflammation of the pancreas. The most common signs are abdominal pain, depression, decreased appetite, vomiting, and diarrhea. In severe cases there may be shock or total collapse. Pancreatitis is diagnosed by a blood test and is a medical emergency. Treatment is pain control, fluid therapy, antibiotics, and dietary changes once the dog recovers. Dogs can get chronic pancreatitis as well.

PATELLAR LUXATION

Patellar luxation occurs when the kneecap moves out of position. It often occurs in both knees. This is easily diagnosed by your vet by manipulating the kneecap. Symptoms can vary from lameness to complete inability to bear weight; in some cases there are no symptoms at all. Surgery is a highly successful treatment.

REVERSE SNEEZING

Reverse sneezing is not really an illness, but it can be alarming the first time you see it. This involves short periods (one to two minutes) of severe air hunger, or snorting. Sometimes irritation of the nasal passages from dust or allergens can be the cause. It can happen every few days, once a week... once a month. The "cure" is to make the dog swallow by massaging the upper throat area or by briefly closing the two little openings in the nose. Relief should come almost immediately.

COMPLEMENTARY AND NATURAL MEDICINE

Complementary and holistic (or natural) medicines are fields that are rapidly expanding in both human and veterinary practices. Therapies include acupuncture, chiropractic, physical therapy, massage therapy, nutrition, herbal medicine, and homeopathy. Complementary practitioners combine the best of natural therapies along with conventional medicine. A holistically oriented veterinarian may look at other possible causes of disease such as environmental conditions, nutritional deficiencies, potential vaccine reactions, etc. Many holistic practitioners use the term "animal companions" or "animal caretakers" rather than "animal owners."

In order to find a holistic veterinarian, contact the American Holistic Veterinary Medical Association at www.ahvma.org.

FIRST AID

Despite our best efforts, emergencies do happen. It's best to be prepared in case anything harmful happens to your Shih Tzu.

POISON

Some items in your household can be poison to your dog. Just one lick of sweet-tasting antifreeze can be fatal, as can herbicides, insecticides, some types of mulch, and other outdoor products. Chocolate contains theobromine, a stimulant that can affect the central nervous system as well as heart muscle. Onions, raisins, grapes, macadamia nuts, mushrooms, and the artificial sweetener Xylitol are also hazardous.

Some common plants should be kept out of reach, including lily of the valley, azalea, yew, rhododendron, shamrock, hibiscus, philodendron, and hydrangea. Certain varieties of mushrooms can cause liver damage or other illnesses.

If your dog ingests anything harmful, call your veterinarian or the ASPCA Animal Poison Control Center at 1-888-426-4435 (a consultation fee may apply). Be prepared to state your pet's breed, age, weight, and any symptoms. Keep the substance with you to help the operator make treatment recommendations.

ALLERGIC REACTIONS

Dogs can have allergic reactions (anaphylaxis) to insect bites, medications, and certain foods and plants. The signs of anaphylaxis are the same as those from a vaccine reaction (see section on Vaccinations above). If you know your dog has an allergy to an item you may not be able to avoid, ask your vet about keeping epinephrine on hand. Your vet can give you a prescription and show you how to use it.

FIRST AID KIT

The American Veterinary Medical Association has a printable list of first aid items to keep handy

Some basic knowledge of first aid could help make the difference to your Shih Tzu in case of emergency.

at www.avma.org/firstaid/supplies.asp, along with a very thorough first aid discussion.

Always remember that any first aid administered to your pet should be followed by immediate veterinary care.

SENIOR CITIZEN SHIH TZU

Smaller breeds like the Shih Tzu mature faster than larger breeds, but they age more slowly after reaching maturity. Small dogs usually aren't considered "geriatric" until they are at least ten years old. It isn't unusual to see a Shih Tzu still in very good health at age 15 or 16— even older.

As the senior years approach it is necessary to increase your dog's annual veterinarian visits to every six months. Be sure to let your vet know if there have been changes in behavior, more frequent urination, loss of appetite, or any other sign of impending ill health. He may begin to have vision problems or trouble with the steps. Also discuss the pros and cons of putting your Shih Tzu on a senior food or other specialized food based on his health needs.

BE AWARE!

Time is critical if you think your dog has been poisoned. Call your veterinarian or the ASPCA Animal Poison Control Center at 1-888-426-4435. Be prepared to state your dog's breed, age, weight, and symptoms. Have the item with you to help them make recommendations.

COGNITIVE DYSFUNCTION

The senior dog often begins to show a different side to his personality. One cause may be cognitive dysfunction, also known as "doggy Alzheimer's."

A dog suffering from dementia may:
• start sleeping during the day and stay awake at night
• appear more anxious
• have a loss of appetite
• bark for no reason, especially at night
• not greet you or recognize you
• get lost in the yard or house
• soil in the house
• become timid or aggressive

There are several treatment options for cognitive dysfunction. Your veterinarian may prescribe the following:
• Anipryl, also used in humans for treatment of Alzheimer's disease, is expensive, but is available in generic form as selegiline. Some dog owners report great

improvement in their pet, others not so much. Read the label carefully so you can distinguish between any side effects and normal decline in the dog's behavior.

- A prescription diet rich in antioxidants may help with an improvement in learning ability, recognition of family members, alertness, and increased attentiveness to problem-solving tasks.

The following medications are available without a prescription, but you should check with your veterinarian before you use them:

- Novifit, a form of SAMe, works by maintaining neurotransmitter function.
- Senilife may promote cognitive health and slow the process of decline through the use of antioxidants, including resveratrol.
- Cholodin, a dietary supplement, contains amino acids, vitamins, and trace minerals such as zinc and selenium. It is formulated to aid senior pets in the improvement of hearing, memory, muscle tone, alertness, and hair coat.

INCONTINENCE

Older females can experience loss of bladder sphincter tone and "leak." The most common treatment is phenylpropanolamine (PPA), which causes the muscles to contract. It works in as many as 90 percent of dogs. Estrogen supplementation works about 60 percent of the time.

There is a surgical procedure in which the bladder is actually repositioned to reduce dribbling. A procedure involving collagen injections can narrow the diameter of the urethra in some cases.

Bladder stones or tumors, urinary tract infections, Cushing's disease, diabetes, and failing kidneys should be ruled out. Also consider that this may be a behavior problem. Older dogs may become more dependent on their owners and may urinate when excited to see them.

OTHER AGING ISSUES
Cancer

Aging is the single leading risk factor in the development of cancer. Watch for any abnormalities in your dog such as lumps, weight loss, difficulty eating, loss of stamina, difficulty in breathing, and any unusual bleeding or discharge. Once a diagnosis is made, you and your vet can determine the treatment based on other illnesses and how well the dog gets along in general. There have been significant advancements in canine cancer treatment, so there is plenty of hope. Ultimately, the key to a good prognosis is early detection.

Behavior Change

An otherwise sweet, happy dog may become aggressive as he ages. This could be the result of a medical problem that causes pain (arthritis or disk degeneration), vision or hearing loss, or lack of mobility. Stresses such as moving, a new family member, or a new pet may make an older dog more irritable.

Once your dog gets a clean bill of health, see whether a refresher course in easy obedience commands will help him rejuvenate. Give him plenty of praise and treats. Using a leash or even a halter in the house may provide more control, especially if he has decreased hearing or vision. Make sure he has stable footing and bedding he can easily get into.

It is possible he needs more mental stimulation or just more attention to reduce his anxiety, especially if he is blind or deaf. Try not to leave him home alone as much. Revisit that bond you built with him as a puppy or young adult! There will come a time when you will be very glad you spent that extra time with him.

A Shih Tzu becomes a senior around 10 years old.

TRAINING
YOUR SHIH TZU

While small dogs like the Shih Tzu tend to get away with a little more than large dogs do, they still need to learn to be good canine citizens. A well-trained dog is more likely to be included when you have company and go on family outings. And, in addition to having a socially acceptable pet, you will be a socially acceptable dog owner!

Chances are the dog's breeder spent a great deal of time playing with the litter, doing basic housetraining, and exposing them to stimuli. The breeder can fill you in on the puppy's personality type and what he has learned so far. If you are fortunate enough to have a puppy from such a breeder, continue with his education. If this was not the case, it is certainly not too late, even if your Shih Tzu is an older dog. The key is to begin right away and give the dog the time and attention he deserves.

The puppy or adult dog needs to learn the rules of the household from the start. What are his toilet options? Which toys are his and which ones belong to the humans? What pieces of furniture can he snooze on, if any? Everyone in the family needs to learn the rules, too, and help the new family member adapt.

Shih Tzu can be very stubborn, so keep that in mind while training. Just be firm and don't let your dog outsmart you with that loving face. A dog who is well trained is much easier to groom and play with than one who is spoiled!

A BRIEF HISTORY OF TRAINING

There are numerous references to man training dogs throughout history, particularly in the past 300 years. Sporting and hunting dog masters would meet and share their breeding and training methods, and many were published in popular magazines and newspapers of the time.

More recently, pets and show dogs have entered the obedience arena. Unfortunately, at first many trainers tended to use harsh methods like jerking or popping the leash, or even dragging a dog

Positive, reward-based methods are the best way to train your Shih Tzu.

to force him to heel. The Koehler Method, named for William Koehler, was based on negative reinforcement and punishment, with the understanding that the dog does what you want him to do in order to escape an unpleasant experience. More than 40,000 dogs were trained at his school in the 1950s and 1960s. Other harsh methods included hanging the dog by his leash and the alpha roll, where the dog is forcibly put on his back or side until he submits. But at what cost was this type of training to the dogs? Instead of making a dog learn by force or fear, why not give him the skills he needs to learn and remain happy and confident at the same time?

POSITIVE REINFORCEMENT

The tide began to turn as methods emerged using positive rather than negative reinforcement. Trainers and behaviorists began to take a look at operant conditioning, which originated in 1938 with B.F. Skinner. In his "Skinner Box" experiments, he changed the behavior of rats by giving them a food reward when they pressed a lever. The theory explains the functional relationship between environmental events and behavior, a key to how living things learn. That is, there is a consequence for the dog's actions—teaching him to think about his choices and choose behavior that pays rewards. It seems many dog trainers and pet owners had been using this method for many years, but just did not have a name for it.

In 1975, William Campbell's *Behavior Problems in Dogs* provided solutions to a whole range of problem behaviors a dog may exhibit. The book became a reference for scores of animal behaviorists, trainers, and veterinarians, considering such factors as family dynamics, the dog's age and medical condition, the environment, and nutrition.

In the past 20 years, veterinarian and animal behaviorist Dr. Ian Dunbar has promoted a positive motivational training method using food rewards. His methods are user friendly and have been adapted by many pet owners. In helping found the Association of Pet Dog Trainers (APDT) in 1993, and with numerous public and television appearances, he has shown a remarkable ability to promote positive training.

In 1984, Karen Pryor published *Don't Shoot the Dog*, an explanation of operant conditioning for the general public. Pryor is best known for developing clicker training, which uses a small plastic device that makes a short distinct "click" sound that tells the animals exactly when they're doing the right thing. Combined with positive reinforcement, this is an effective, safe, and humane way to teach any animal any behavior it is physically and mentally capable of doing.

TRAINING DO'S AND DON'TS

- Regardless of which positive method you use, remember that consistency is the most important rule in training a dog. He will get confused if one family member says "off" the couch and another says "down." Keep a list of the commands you have decided to use so everyone can use the same words.
- Verbal reprimands are not the same as verbally abusing your dog. Reprimands are necessary to stop the unwanted behavior. The reprimand can be delivered in a firm, deep voice to distinguish it from your normal speech. Reprimands should not be given with emotion or anger.
- Never hit your dog. When you influence behavior without force, the dog's trust in his human will be stronger.
- Time outs can be effective for dogs as long as they are not for a long period of time. If you use your dog's crate for time out, he can start thinking of it as punishment, not his safe haven. Or using the crate for time out could backfire if he enjoys being there and simply decides to take a nap. Find a place for him to stay, removed from the situation and removed from his family, but not for so long that he will feel abandoned.
- Ignoring a behavior like begging at the table can make the dog go away and not try again. Or it may make him try in other ways to get food, like scratching or whining. It is hard to resist a dog who tries so hard for any type of reward, but if you persevere, ignoring him should eventually work.

HOUSETRAINING

The first thing you will want to do when you bring your new puppy or adult home is teach him potty manners. Even if his breeder or former owner trained him, he still needs to know the new rules. He may even rebel somewhat from being in a new home and need some gentle reminders.

USING A CRATE

An effective way to housetrain your dog is by using a crate. Not only does the crate allow you to supervise your Shih Tzu, but dogs don't like to soil where they sleep, so your puppy will naturally avoid eliminating in the crate. Crate training works because the puppy learns that when the urge to urinate or defecate occurs, he can hold it.

First, choose a crate that allows your dog to lie down comfortably, stand up, and easily turn around. If the crate is too large, he might soil one end of it and sleep at the other. If you have a crate of the right size and your puppy ends up soiling the crate, you'll need to rethink your schedule and take him out more often.

Line the crate with a blanket or a dog bed, put in some treats or a toy, and then entice the puppy to get in. Once he has figured out how to go in and out of his crate, use a cue word such as "Bed" as he moves toward the crate, and hand him a treat once he is inside. Repeat this several times at random until he goes in when he's told to. Then get him accustomed to being in the crate with the door closed, praising him as needed.

During the housetraining period you can use the crate during the night by carrying it into your bedroom so you can hear your puppy's pleas to go outside. Or you can purchase a second crate for the bedroom. You can also use the crate if you're away during the day—but not more than a few hours at a time. If you have to be away from home for a longer period of time, you should find someone to give your Shih Tzu a potty break while you are gone. The dog needs to see the crate as a personal refuge or a nice cozy place to take a nap. It should not be used as a way to confine your Shih Tzu for a long term.

If for some reason you prefer not to use a crate, you can try paper training your puppy.

THE HOUSETRAINING PROCESS

Consistency and close supervision are keys to housetraining your Shih Tzu.

To start, always keep an eye on your dog for signs he needs to go outside, such as whining, circling, sniffing, barking, or scratching. Don't let him run around the house—get him outside right away. At the door, ask "Outside?" then as you go out, repeat "Outside." Go with him and watch to make sure he takes care of business. You may want to train him to go to a certain part of the yard for your convenience in cleaning up. And be sure to reward him for going in the right place. The best times to take him outside are when he first wakes up, after meals, after playing, after napping, and after he has been in his crate for a while.

PAPER TRAINING

If you prefer not to use a crate, you can section off a small area in a laundry room or bathroom and use the same principle as crate training. Many people use newspapers or piddle pads in the area, making the available "spot" smaller and closer to the door as the puppy gets older, and eventually taking the papers away altogether. This method was used for a long time before crate training caught on, so it can work. Just be aware of what your puppy is doing and watch out for signs that he has to go out. By the way, newspapers may not be a good choice for a light-colored dog, as the ink will rub off on the dog. See whether you can buy newsprint (without ink) by the roll instead.

Some owners of small dogs opt to use piddle pads or newspapers throughout the life of the dog. In some cases, like apartment living, this may be necessary,

Never punish your puppy for a housetraining accident.

and with travel it can be a real convenience. Piddle pads have a non-skid plastic backing, absorbent layers, and leakproof edges. Some are scented so dogs will be attracted to them. You can buy a plastic bed to anchor the pad in. There are even dog litter boxes and sod systems for indoor pottying.

Think indoor training out carefully, because once the behavior goes on for a period of time it may be difficult to change. And it is no substitute for taking your dog for a nice long walk. That walk is good for both of you!

ACCIDENTS HAPPEN
Don't punish your puppy if he has an accident. If you catch him in the act, tell him gently that he is a bad boy and take him outside. When he has been good, praise him enthusiastically or give him a treat.

If you find a mess on the floor, clean it up and forget it. Unless you catch him in the act, he will have no idea what the scolding is for. He doesn't have the capacity to put the punishment together with something he has done without incident numerous times before, especially if he did it more than a few minutes ago.

Try to clean the area thoroughly so he will not be attracted to the smell and go there again. This will be more difficult on carpets, but try your best. There are some enzyme-based cleaners that claim to get rid of the smell completely.

HOW LONG?
It is hard to say how long a healthy dog will take to housetrain. A Shih Tzu has a smaller bladder than a larger dog, so allow several months until he's reliable.

If your puppy seems to have a particularly difficult time with his housetraining, make sure there is no health problem like a urinary tract infection or a kidney problem. A urinalysis and blood panel may be necessary.

SOCIALIZATION
Socialization is the exposure to different environments, learning to interact acceptably with humans and other animals, and the opportunity for exploration. Puppies are capable of learning at an incredibly quick pace, so you should expose your Shih Tzu to as many (safe) stimuli as possible, just as you would a human child. This will help your puppy grow up to be a friendly, confident, reliable, and happy member of your family.

When your Shih Tzu first comes home with you, he needs an introduction to his new kingdom. It's best not to overwhelm him with too many activities and new people. Take it gradually—there is plenty of time. And until he has had his puppy vaccinations, avoid any high-risk areas like dog parks, the sidewalk and parking lot of your vet's office, and the vet's waiting room floor. Once your puppy has been sufficiently vaccinated, it should be safe to take him to more public places.

In the meantime, make sure he meets as many people as possible in his home or in other safe places. Ideally, he should meet people of all ages—children, the elderly, people who use canes, etc. Ask your guests to sit on the floor if they can and let the puppy go to them. He will probably want to sniff their hands and maybe even do a little dance to show off. This is his time to shine—to bask in all the attention, learn new smells and voices. He should thoroughly enjoy this play time.

Socialization also means that puppies (and adult dogs) experience loud noises and strange sounds such as vacuum cleaners, dishwashers, music, doorbells, and other household sounds. When your puppy is first exposed to such a noise, make a happy, playful sound and play with him so he will associate the noise with something positive. Chances are he will come to ignore these sounds, (except for the doorbell, which tends to cause a frenzy in even the most socialized dog).

Be sure to expose your puppy to different surfaces as well. His first time in the grass can be scary. But enticing him with a treat or a squeaky toy can make him forget all about the grass tickling his paws.

Properly socialized, your Shih Tzu should be able to get along with other dogs.

You'll want your Shih Tzu to be able to go places with you, so he needs to get accustomed to car rides. If you noticed your puppy was afraid in the car ride bringing him home or to the vet, have someone soothe him or play with him (in his crate or airline bag) while you are driving.

PUPPY KINDERGARTEN

The 8 to 16 weeks of age period is a critical developmental stage for puppies. Puppy kindergarten classes are a great way for your dog to learn how to handle new situations and increase his social skills, as well as help you learn how to prevent problems from turning into serious issues as the dog matures.

BE AWARE! Be consistent! This is the most important rule in training a dog. Your Shih Tzu will get confused if one family member says "Off" the couch and another says "Down." Keep a list of the commands you have decided on so everyone can use the same words.

Before you enroll, find out what the teaching philosophy of the instructor is. You will want to be comfortable with his or her methods of training. Small class size is important so that your puppy will get plenty of individual attention, if needed. You will want to choose a class that spends an appropriate amount of time teaching and not just letting the puppies play for most of the session.

At this early age make sure proof of vaccination is required of all attendees, since your puppy's classmates will be unfamiliar dogs. Visiting a class prior to enrollment is a good way to determine whether this is the kindergarten for your puppy.

BASIC COMMANDS

Training a puppy (as well as an adult) can be fun as well as exasperating. Shih Tzu can be a little stubborn, so you may have to make yours think the behaviors you want are all his idea. Make him think he is the one who initiated the act and praise him.

Unless you plan to train your dog for the obedience ring, small pieces of cheese, hot dog, dried liver, or whatever he likes can be used to entice him to learn. (Food is not allowed in the obedience ring.) Vary the treat to keep it interesting. You can buy small bags to attach to your belt to keep your treats in to help facilitate giving the reward in a timely way. If you prefer to reward your Shih Tzu with praise, this works very well, too. Some dogs are just as happy with that extra special attention.

Vary the location where you practice the exercises. Your dog may stay perfectly in your kitchen, but may find too many distractions in other environments. Try the back yard, near playgrounds, and the park. Make sure he is always on his leash if the area is not enclosed, even if you think he will stay with you. You never know what distractions may make him run off to explore. And be aware of other dogs who show interest in your dog, as they may pose a threat.

Teaching your dog basic commands—*sit, down, stay, come, leave it,* and *heel*—will help your dog become a great pet. Three of these basic obedience commands—*down, come,* and *leave it*—could literally save your dog's life. Once these behaviors are learned, you will be surprised at how eager your Shih Tzu will be to show off for you and your guests.

SIT

The *sit* command is useful to keep your dog from jumping up on a visitor, or to make him sit still at the vet's office or at a photo shoot. You can start training your dog to sit when he sits on his own. When you see him sit, say, "Sit!" immediately and praise and give him a treat. See how you can make him think this was all his idea? Eventually he should sit for longer periods of time.

Otherwise, you can use a food lure to teach the command. Hold a treat in front of your Shih Tzu's nose, then slowly raise it over his head—not too far, you don't want him jumping for it. When he sits, say "Good Sit" and give him the reward.

A reliable *down* command can help keep your Shih Tzu safe in case he ever breaks loose from his collar.

At home, incorporate the sit command into your daily routine. Ask your dog to sit before you feed him or get him to sit before you throw his ball at the park. When you have a clever and crafty dog like a Shih Tzu, it never hurts to teach him early that he needs to earn his keep.

If you plan to try your hand at obedience trials, shoot for a one-minute sit and you will be ahead of the pack when your dog starts school. Remember that food rewards are not permitted in most formal obedience classes and never in the obedience ring.

DOWN

Why is training in the *down* command important? Let's say your worst fear comes true and your Shih Tzu breaks loose from his collar and gets away. You see him nearing a busy street. Your heart is pounding and you immediately yell "Down!" Your well-trained Shih Tzu goes down and stays there until you can get to him and put his collar back on. By training him to obey this command, you can help ensure your dog's safety.

You can teach your dog the *down* command by rewarding the behavior whenever he lies down on his own. When you see him lie down, immediately say "Down!" then praise and reward him.

Another way to train him in the *down* is to entice him into a down position with a treat. Hold a treat in front of his nose and bring it to the floor. He should follow it, and when his body is on the floor, reward him with the treat. Repeat as often as you need to until he is able to obey the command, but not so much he gets bored and tired. Never push him down, only gently guide him if necessary.

As he gets the hang of it, you can have him stay in the *down* for longer periods of time. If you have plans to train your dog in obedience, work on having him stay down for three minutes (the requirement for the first level, Novice A). And you'll have to omit the treats or wean him off them if you plan to compete.

Down can be a confusing command because some dog owners will use it to mean "get off the couch," or "stop jumping on me," as well as "lie down." Make sure everyone in the family uses the term properly so your dog will not be confused.

STAY

Once your dog has mastered the *sit* or *down*, the next important command is the *stay*. The *sit* and *down* commands aren't of much value if your dog merely gets into those positions and then bounces back up! When you think about it, though, asking your dog to stay goes against his natural instinct, which is to follow you.

Begin teaching this command after a walk when he is calm, and in an area where there are no distractions. Have your dog sit in front of you, using the *sit* command. Place your palm near his face and say "Stay." If he stays in his current position, even for a few seconds, praise him. Then, with your dog in a sit, try taking a step away from him, then come right back and reward him if he didn't move. Then stay back in longer increments. You may want to start with two seconds and gradually increase up to ten seconds. If he moves, don't praise or reward him. After a few attempts, he should start to realize that when he does not move, he will be rewarded.

This same procedure can be applied to train your dog to stay in the *down* position. Once he has learned to stay in either position, repeat the command from a distance, moving farther away as he progresses.

The *stay* is a great command to use when visitors come to your home or if you have a dog who likes to take off. This can be a lifesaving command if your dog is ever in harm's way at a distance and you need for him to stay where he is.

COME (RECALL)

As in the *down* scenario, a *come* command could work if your dog gets loose and is in an area where it is safe for him to run back to you.

Teach your Shih Tzu to come in a safely enclosed area.

The *come*, known as the *recall* in obedience training, should be taught in a safely enclosed area. Place your dog in a *sit-stay* and walk a few feet (m) away. Say "Come!" and take a few steps back. Use a squeaky toy, treat, or amusing noises, whatever it takes to make him come to you. Praise him enthusiastically. Repeat and gradually increase the distance between you.

This exercise can also be taught with the dog on a long leash for better control. You can use the leash to gently guide your dog to you, but *do not* pop or pull it. Or try squatting down and opening your arms to him.

If your dog is stubborn and will not come when you ask him to, or you have called him away from a dangerous situation, never punish him. Go to the dog, put on his leash, guide him back to where you called him from, and praise him. This teaches the dog that he must follow the command, but that you are not angry. Your dog must always think coming to you is a happy, safe, wonderful thing to experience.

LEAVE IT

Occasionally you may drop something on the floor that could be harmful to your dog, such as medication, a battery, a hot cooking utensil, or human food that may be toxic to your Shih Tzu. Or you may be on a walk in the park and come across something unsavory that your dog thinks looks yummy. Dogs just don't know what is good for them. In these instances, the *leave it* command will stop your dog from getting into anything dangerous.

Start by putting your dog on a short leash and dropping a "good" treat on the floor. As he starts for the treat, say "Leave It!" Reward him immediately with a better treat and praise him. Gradually increase the time before he gets the good treat, and eventually train him without his leash. For best results, practice in various locations where he may come across something he shouldn't have.

HEEL

Heeling on leash is one of the most useful behaviors a good dog can have. It will help you navigate crowds and keep your dog from roaming into the path of others, and from sniffing everything in sight.

Heel means your dog walks nicely on his leash by your side. In formal obedience, the dog walks on your left side, not your right side, so you might want to practice this way if you plan to compete.

Hold your dog's leash in your right hand; while taking up its slack in your left, tell him to "Sit!" Then hold a treat in your left hand, and say "Heel!" in a bouncy voice. Walk briskly for about ten paces, keeping the food slightly elevated at your

Walking nicely on leash is one of the most useful behaviors a dog can have.

side. Slowly stop and lift the treat slightly or pull up on the leash so that your dog sits. Then reward him.

If you want to wean your dog off food rewards in case something happens away from home and you are empty-handed, start rewarding him with lots of praise along with the treat, then give the treat intermittently. Or give him the "Heel" command and occasionally walk over to the cookie jar to get him a treat. He will want to obey "in case" he gets the reward.

INCREASE THE DIFFICULTY

Once your dog is able to obey these basic commands, increase his skill level by having him sit or stay down for a longer period of time, or come from a farther distance away. Add distractions like having other people walk around, talk, and maybe even call him away from you. If he likes to chase balls, have someone bounce one in the same room. Your job is to train him, not trick him, so make his road to success as easy as possible. The key is consistency, adding new tasks gradually, and giving plenty of rewards for good behavior.

FINDING A PROFESSIONAL TRAINER

Check with a kennel club or obedience club in your area to see whether they hold puppy kindergarten or socialization classes. A pet store or private trainer may offer classes as well. The Association of Pet Dog Trainers (APDT) is another

Dog Tale

When you train your Shih Tzu, keep in mind that your method has to be adjusted to his individual temperament. I've learned with my own dogs that not every dog reacts the same way. By learning each individual dog's body language I can anticipate how that dog will react.

great source for positive trainers. This organization was founded in 1993 by Dr. Ian Dunbar, a renowned veterinarian, animal behaviorist, dog trainer, and writer. The mission of APDT is to promote caring relationships between dogs and people by educating trainers in canine behavior and emphasizing professionalism and reward-based training. You can find a trainer near you at their website: www.apdt.com.

Some trainers address problem behaviors, others simply offer obedience exercises. You will be able to tell during the first class whether the trainer uses positive reinforcement methods. Or sit in on a few classes before you enroll. Although the Shih Tzu is a solid, sturdy dog, he is still a small dog. He is a creature who thrives on attention and pleasing his human. There is no need for negative training techniques when positive methods are much more humane and so much fun to do.

Many people who sign up for one class enjoy the experience so much they become involved in obedience trials and go on for American Kennel Club (AKC) or United Kennel Club (UKC) titles. Others branch into conformation showing as the "show" bug hits them. You may have the opportunity to meet someone in the classes who can guide you in this direction, or perhaps your Shih Tzu breeder is involved in the sport.

Training your Shih Tzu can be fun for both of you, whether you do it yourself, attend obedience classes, or use a private trainer. It is possible to prepare your dog without a trainer, but it is much better for both of you to attend classes where you will have distractions, constructive criticism, and plenty of socialization. You will be amazed at your dog's potential to learn and the bond it will create between the two of you. The ultimate goal is a well-adjusted, happy family member.

SOLVING PROBLEMS
WITH YOUR
SHIH TZU

Behavioral problems are the largest single cause of dog abandonment, relinquishment to shelters, and premature euthanasia in the United States. Behaviors such as barking, chewing, house soiling, jumping up, and nipping can be problematic—and, sadly, many dog owners are not willing to take the necessary steps to control the behaviors and save their family pet.

Take heart. Old dogs (and young dogs) can be taught new tricks. Most of these behaviors can be corrected with a little patience and training. Many of them are a matter of the dog's simply not getting adequate training.

The first thing to consider is whether there is an obvious cause for the problem behavior. Let's say your housetrained Shih Tzu suddenly begins having accidents in the house. Is your dog soiling because he is left too long without being let outside or walked? Or, if the behavior began suddenly, could he have a bladder infection, or should his kidneys be checked? An underlying medical issue may be the cause of a change in behavior, so have your Shih Tzu checked out by his vet.

Another common cause of problems such as jumping up, barking, and chewing is lack of adequate attention. Shih Tzu, and dogs in general, are very social animals. They want to be part of the action, and often they will exhibit unacceptable behavior if they don't get enough attention.

Positive reinforcement techniques, as discussed in Chapter 7, can be applied to a dog who is misbehaving. These techniques show the dog there is a consequence for his actions—that he needs to think about his choices and choose the behavior that pays a reward. Keep in mind that positive reinforcement does not mean the dog is never corrected. It simply means that adding something positive, like a treat or praise, will increase the likelihood that a good behavior will recur.

Dog Tale

Our six-year-old Shih Tzu rescue, Tinkerbell, came to us very afraid of men. We wondered if a man had injured her or scared her in the past. So, we decided to try to get her over her fear in a positive, stress-free way. We had some friends come over, and we all sat on the floor and let her visit us on her own. She stayed away from our male friend but he did not try to interact with her. He ignored her while she interacted with the rest of us. After some time, Tinkerbell got curious and decided she wanted to interact with him, too. He fed her some tasty treats for approaching him. With time and gentle socialization, she became less wary of men.

AGGRESSION

Aggressive behavior is not normal in the Shih Tzu, but it is not unheard of. There could be a medical cause, the dog could have been abused at some point, or he could be a product of poor breeding. The owner's behavior, such as teasing or excessive punishment, could also contribute.

Aggression can be toward strangers, toward the owner, toward other animals, or even toward certain groups of people or one of the sexes. Types of aggression include fear, territorial, possessive, and dominance.

The first thing to do is rule out any medical cause for the aggression. Hypothyroidism has been known to cause aggression in dogs. If this is the case, the typical signs of the disease are usually not present, such as skin or coat problems, lethargy, or weight gain. The dog is simply "grumpy" or unwilling to share the sofa with you. Medication will bring a marked improvement in the behavior.

A toothache, joint pain, and even eye pain can cause biting. More serious conditions like encephalitis, epilepsy, distemper, a brain tumor, or head trauma should be considered, especially if the aggression started suddenly. As in humans, low serotonin levels in the brain are known to cause abnormal behavior. This brain neurotransmitter is responsible for our sense of well-being,

Once your vet has ruled out any medical cause for the aggression, the only option is to learn how to manage the behavior with help from a professional. This

Some problem behaviors may be the result of lack of attention or boredom.

is a very complex subject (beyond the scope of this book), but you should know that many aggressive behaviors can be managed, even unlearned. Others are ingrained in the dog forever and, sadly, some aggressive dogs cannot be helped. When it comes to aggression, you must seek help from a trainer or a behaviorist—for your dog's sake and for the well-being of other people and animals.

BARKING

Having served as watchdogs for so many centuries, Shih Tzu can be real barkers. They generally are not yappy barkers—their barking is more self-important and alerting. Wolves and other wild canids bark very little. Through domestication, we may have created a companion who barks more than what meets our modern needs.

Unfortunately, barking is not only one of the most annoying behaviors, it's also one of the most difficult behaviors to control. It can cause a problem with your neighbors, difficulty getting to sleep at night, or commotion when someone rings the doorbell. Persistent barking is not good for your dog either, as it could be causing him stress.

Sometimes we create the problem by rewarding barking unknowingly. When the very young puppy starts barking, we think it is charming and with this encouragement he barks more. Then he barks to demand attention, and we still think it's cute. Eventually, he learns that all he has to do to get attention is bark. After all, this is his main form of communication, so how can it be so wrong?

Not all of this "communication" is wanted or appreciated by friends or family, not to mention the neighbors. The key to dealing with excessive barking is to be able to turn it off.

Having served as watchdogs for so many centuries, Shih Tzu can be real barkers.

WHY IS HE BARKING?

Your Shih Tzu may make various sounds, including barking, howling, whining, whimpering, and yelping. There are many reasons for barking, and some can be resolved more quickly than others.

- Is he trying to get you to play, or just trying to get your attention? If you have time to play, by all means do so. He may not be getting enough exercise or mental stimulation. If you simply do not have time to play, offer him a toy and encourage him to play.
- Does he have to go O-U-T? If so, think about your housetraining schedule and try to provide him with more opportunities to relieve himself.
- Is he frustrated because he can't get his toy out from under the sofa? This one's easy—retrieve it for him!
- Is he in pain or discomfort? See your vet to find out whether there's a health issue involved.
- Is another dog in the house or neighborhood striking up a "conversation" and he's just joining in? Again a distraction such as a toy or treat may work; if not, it may come under the category of "alert barking" (see below).

CURBING ALERT BARKING

Alert barking, which your Shih Tzu is a pro at, can be a good thing when you have a not-so-welcome visitor. Dogs have prevented plenty of burglaries. But when your Shih Tzu carries on every time someone sets foot on your property, the noise and accompanying behavior become a nuisance.

For this type of barking, train him to accept "good dog" or "thank you" for performing his duty when he first begins to bark. Say it curtly so he will stop barking. If this does not work, use "Stop it!" or "Enough!" and give him a reward after he has stopped for five seconds or so. This may take quite a few tries before it works, so be patient.

COMPULSIVE BARKING

More serious barking behaviors may require the assistance of a behaviorist. Compulsive barking is repetitive for long periods of time and is accompanied by pacing, spinning, and so on. It is similar to compulsive behavior in humans. Aggressive barking is where your dog is trying to warn someone away from his territory or protect a family member.

CHEWING

Puppies chew; that is a fact. You need to provide safe, appropriate chew items for your Shih Tzu puppy during this time. Puppies particularly like to chew when they are teething. You can't blame them—their gums are sore. (Even an older dog may start chewing if his gums hurt or if he has a loose tooth.) One solution is to dampen a washcloth, twist it, then place it in the freezer for a few hours. Once it is nice and firm, offer it to the puppy to soothe his gums. Ice chips may also work.

Don't be tempted to give your puppy an old slipper to chew on, even if he insists. He may think all slippers are fair game from then on.

The next step is to prevent him from getting into things you don't want him to have. This means ensuring he does not have access to electrical cords or trash cans. You also need to make sure that items like shoes, socks, papers, prescriptions—anything your puppy is not allowed to have—are picked up and not within his reach.

If you find your puppy chewing on something inappropriate, stop him with a sharp "No!," then offer him something he is allowed to chew, such as a toy or treat. Then reward him for playing with or chewing the new item. When you are not there to monitor him, sprays that leave a bitter flavor on items can work as a deterrent to chewing.

Adult dogs may chew or destroy items out of frustration caused by simple boredom. They do not chew to retaliate—dogs have no concept of spite. Make sure your Shih Tzu has plenty of his own "stuff" to play with, and spend time playing with and exercising him. Make his life as full as possible to cut down on any boredom or frustration.

Don't be tempted to give your puppy an old slipper to chew on—he may think all slippers are fair game from then on.

COPROPHAGIA

Coprophagia is the practice of eating stool (feces). It is not an abnormal behavior to the dog. Dams routinely do it while keeping their puppies clean. It is a normal way for young puppies to explore their environment. Most puppies eventually learn that food tastes better and have absolutely no interest in this behavior.

Your vet should rule out any medical problems for the behavior, such as pancreatic enzyme insufficiency, malabsorption (difficulty absorbing nutrients from food), or poor diet. And his stool should be checked for parasites.

Occasionally, coprophagia is just a lifelong banquet for the dog. It is a very difficult behavior to change, unless you have just one dog and can be with him at the right time. Some dog owners get results by changing the diet or adding meat tenderizer or papaya to the food to help increase protein digestion, resulting in a less edible stool. You can sprinkle the feces with hot sauce in hopes that he doesn't like a more spicy diet. Try adding more fiber to his diet or switch to a "free feed" regimen so he always has something to eat.

You can try training the dog to sit for a special treat immediately following each bowel movement, and maybe this will become a permanent habit. Another option is to try a "Leave it!" command and then clean up the area quickly.

DIGGING

The Shih Tzu is certainly not a breed with strong digging instincts, like the terrier, but anything is possible when you have a canine in the household. Dogs dig out of boredom. They dig to escape or, if unneutered, they may want to dig under the fence on a quest for a mate. Maybe they are trying to hide a toy or bone. Watch your dog closely until you determine the reason he may be digging.

Dirt is not the Shih Tzu's friend. The last thing you need is to find your bundle of joy covered in dirt or mud. To prevent this, a small edging fence will keep him away from the most tempting places to dig. There are also items (like ground hot chili peppers) that you can spread over the soil that are not harmful to your dog, but the nasty taste may provide a deterrent. Avoid using fertilizer containing bone meal, as this will just attract your dog and encourage digging.

In addition to prevention methods, supervise your Shih Tzu when he's outside. You should never leave your Shih Tzu outside unattended, so this should be easy. Don't punish your dog if you catch him digging; just redirect him to a more appropriate behavior. Focus more on helping him learn what you *want* him to do, rather than what not to do. Play with him in the yard and give him other things to do, like playing with his outside toys.

If you adopt an adult dog who has not been housetrained, start the training from scratch.

HOUSESOILING

Sometimes we are so anxious for our Shih Tzu to be housetrained, we give him a little too much credit and the accidents start again. If this happens, simply start at the beginning with your training, using the crate if you need to. Be particularly aware of any cue that he has to go outside so you can take the opportunity to really praise him for being good.

If you adopt an adult dog who has not been housetrained, start the training from scratch—just as you would a puppy (see Chapter 7). Even if you have been told the dog is housetrained, teach him right away what the rules are for going outside. After all, your environment will be new to him and he will need time to adapt and learn your rules for going outside.

Occasionally, however, an adult dog may have issues that require additional action.

MEDICAL ISSUES

If your dog suddenly begins to have frequent accidents, you need to take him to his vet. Epilepsy can cause involuntary urination or defecation, as can spinal cord injuries and disease. Incontinence is common in older dogs, especially females. The elderly dog who is showing signs of canine cognitive dysfunction, or "doggy Alzheimer's," can start to forget his housetraining. Of course, any number of diseases such as a virus or bacterial infection can cause loose stools or diarrhea. Even puppies can have a medical "excuse" for their behavior. A congenital deformity known as an ectopic ureter, in which the ureter bypasses the bladder, can be corrected by surgery.

MARKING

Male dogs, even if they were neutered at an early age, can still be leg hikers if they were raised around multiple dogs. Leg hiking, or marking, can be territorial or sexual, and has nothing to do with being housetrained. Male urine has pheromones derived from testosterone, which is detected by other dogs—canine "calling cards," so to speak. Sometimes the marking is accompanied by pawing or scratching to define the territory. Your male is showing you this is his house. If your dog has not been neutered, do so immediately. This can help in some cases, but unfortunately, male dogs may still mark if they are stressed or frustrated, such as when they are near female dogs in heat or they are upset by visitors. Also, dominant dogs are more likely to mark if they have an exaggerated sense of importance, as some small male dogs do!

Dominant females may mark, too, so don't be surprised to see your female lift her leg or briefly squat. Females produce small quantities of testosterone in

Marking can be territorial, and has nothing to do with being housetrained.

addition to their own scent that signals their receptivity to mating. Spayed females usually cease this behavior, though occasionally they will urine mark when stressed.

In order to stop this marking, close and consistent supervision is necessary. Confine your dog to one area of the house or use baby gates or an ex-pen. Another option is to put your dog on a leash while he is in the house with you so you will have total control at all times. Reprimand him when he marks in the house, but praise him when he marks in an appropriate place outside, for example a tree or a fire hydrant-shaped stone. (Yes, there is such a thing!) The message is that urine marking isn't bad as long as it is outside, but inside the house isn't a good idea. Basic obedience training is always useful for any housetraining issue.

Belly bands, which wrap around the mid-section, covering the penis, will not stop a dog from hiking, but they do catch the urine if they do. The liner of the belly band needs to be changed as necessary. For females, panties or diapers may act as a deterrent.

As a last resort, it may be necessary to use drug therapy prescribed by your vet. This works by stabilizing the dog's mood, increasing his confidence, or, in females, toning the bladder sphincter. Anxiety-reducing drugs may be effective used simultaneously with training.

So that the dog will not think an area where he has already marked is his own personal space, be sure to clean up the urine marks with an enzymatic or bacterial product that will destroy the odors at the source. Simply masking the scents will not work.

SUBMISSIVE URINATION

Submissive urination is an entirely different situation. These dogs usually wet themselves, or the floor, when you first greet them. They either squat or roll over on their back and dribble, a behavior that dates back to his days as a puppy when

his mother cleaned him. Scolding him only reinforces the behavior and makes it worse. Try ignoring him when you first get home. Be very low key. Let him come to you and have him sniff the palm of your hand. Stoop down gently to his level and pet him under the chin so he will feel calm. Then proceed with letting him out to his yard or walking him. Having your visitors do the same will also help.

JUMPING UP: THE OVERZEALOUS GREETER

Seeing a young puppy jumping up on his hind feet for attention can be very cute. Puppies get very excited about seeing us, and the

Your Shih Tzu may pose to get your attention.

feeling is mutual. We bend down and pick them up, hug them, and kiss them. Our positive reactions end up reinforcing the jumping, and a puppy so treated will soon think this is acceptable behavior. True, a 12-pound (5 kg) Shih Tzu jumping up on a guest is not quite as annoying as a 100-pound (45 kg) dog, but regardless, some guests may not approve. The dog could have muddy paws or, worse, it could be dangerous for a dog to jump on children or the elderly.

In order to stop this overzealous greeting, you need to stop reacting to it. Ignore your dog, avert your eyes, and adopt an indifferent posture. He receives no attention until he stops the behavior. Once he has all four paws on the ground, reward him with a treat. Inform all family members and visitors that this behavior is not permitted, and ask them to follow the same procedure—no attention until your Shih Tzu has stopped jumping. Be consistent. Allowing a jump just one time out of five is enough for your dog to think it is all right after all.

Another positive training method to prevent jumping up is to reward an alternative behavior, like sitting. Train your dog to sit before a visitor comes in, and reward him when he complies. If your dog persists with the jumping, and he is trained to heel and sit, correct him by saying "Off!" and then walk him briskly in a circle, tell him to sit, and reward him. Repeat the exercise as long as it takes for him to understand.

NIPPING AND BITING

Young puppies are very oral. They mouth and chew on their littermates, mother, and everything in sight. While nursing, especially when the puppy teeth begin coming in, some bite too hard and the mother reprimands them with a nip. Littermates will also nip each other as a response to a play bite. This is how a bite inhibition develops in most puppies.

Puppy owners should take advantage of this training from the mother by teaching the puppy that any communication by mouth is unacceptable. No, you don't bite back! You tell the puppy "No!" in a voice slightly louder than your normal voice and ignore him for a few minutes. If this does not work, crate the dog for a short time. Be consistent—follow through *every time* and your puppy

SOLVING PROBLEMS WITH YOUR SHIH TZU

115

will respect your boundaries and stop using his teeth on you. Any visitors who play with you puppy should be told how to do this as well. This is a crucial time to stop mouthing behavior—before the puppy becomes a biting adult.

When it comes to biting, any dog can bite under the right (or wrong) circumstances. Teeth are an important tool to dogs, a way to communicate. If a dog is in pain or feels threatened, he could bite. Different dogs have different pain and threat thresholds. Generally speaking, though, a well-socialized puppy will grow up to be a good canine citizen without biting issues. If, however, you do find your dog biting out of fear or anxiety, seek professional help at once. Biting is a serious issue, even with small dog like the Shih Tzu.

OBSESSIVE COMPULSIVE DISORDER

Although the Shih Tzu is not among the breeds genetically likely to have an obsessive compulsive disorder, the behavior is possible in any breed. With this disorder, the dog performs a behavior over and over, to the extent that it interferes with his normal life. Examples include spinning, pacing, tail chasing, fly snapping, barking, excessive licking, and fence-running. The behavior doesn't seem to have any purpose, but he's compelled to do it anyway.

The dog might lose weight, suffer from exhaustion, and even physically injure himself. Often dogs will learn to control their behavior in the presence of the owner, but then do it when alone. It is very difficult to change.

Sometimes there is no obvious reason for the behavior. Some dogs develop compulsions after having physical conditions that cause them to lick or chew their bodies, such as an injury or allergies. A dog's lifestyle can sometimes contribute if his living conditions cause anxiety or stress, such as dogs who have been abused or have lived penned up in kennels or in puppy mills.

Studies have shown some success

Some dogs simply don't like being alone. Given a choice, they would spend every bit of their time with their humans.

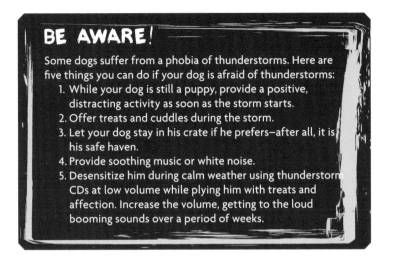

BE AWARE!

Some dogs suffer from a phobia of thunderstorms. Here are five things you can do if your dog is afraid of thunderstorms:

1. While your dog is still a puppy, provide a positive, distracting activity as soon as the storm starts.
2. Offer treats and cuddles during the storm.
3. Let your dog stay in his crate if he prefers—after all, it is his safe haven.
4. Provide soothing music or white noise.
5. Desensitize him during calm weather using thunderstorm CDs at low volume while plying him with treats and affection. Increase the volume, getting to the loud booming sounds over a period of weeks.

using a combination of drugs and behavior modification. Few completely stop the behavior, but have shown improvement. Some dogs respond best to distractions, such as lots of play time or being taken out for a nice long walk. Others respond better to a calmer, more soothing and predictable home environment.

SEPARATION ANXIETY

Having a strong bond with your beloved dog is one of the great joys of life. There are times, however, when you must be apart. Most dogs adapt well to the typical daily separation from their owners. However, if your dog becomes too reliant or dependent on you, he can develop what is called separation anxiety. Some dogs simply don't like being alone. Given a choice, they would spend every bit of their time with their humans.

With separation anxiety, the behavior begins immediately after you leave, usually at the door where you exited or a window where the dog could see you leave. Signs include whining, barking, crying, chewing, scratching the door, salivating, and breaking housetraining. As tempting as it is, you should not go back into the house to try to calm him—it just reinforces the behavior. If you draw out the goodbyes, it makes your leaving more obvious when you are gone.

The first step is to think about what you do as you are preparing to leave. Does your dog recognize that when you pick up your keys or your purse, you are leaving? If so, change your behavior by picking up the keys and perhaps sitting on the couch for a few minutes. Then calmly get up and leave without saying goodbye. Come back inside after a random amount of time, then leave again. When you get home, don't make a big deal about arriving. Condition your dog to thinking your arrivals and departures are not big deals.

Try associating your departures with something positive. As you leave, give your dog a treat. This may take his mind off your leaving. Leave the radio on if he is used to hearing it while you are home. Some dogs will be more relaxed if they can see out a window or door, but others may become even more anxious.

If you set aside time to give your dog undivided attention and plenty of play time, he may be less anxious while you are gone. And if you make his crate or ex-pen area a positive place, this could be your best bet. If he has plenty of room, water, toys, and a soft (indestructible) bed, he could be very happy whiling away the hours until you get home.

WHEN TO CONSULT A BEHAVIORIST

The subject of animal behavior has become increasingly popular in the past ten years or so, with television programming, books, DVDs, and even zoo exhibits.

Working with any behavior problem takes time and patience.

Some behaviorists have become household names. We can learn a lot about how to handle certain behaviors from these media outlets, but nothing surpasses taking your dog to his own personal therapist. If we are not careful, occasionally we may "misdiagnose" our dog's problem and make things worse.

The Animal Behavior Society (ABS) lists Certified Applied Animal Behaviorists on their website (www.animalbehavior.org). These professionals have an advanced graduate degree in animal behavior. Some are veterinarians who have completed a behavioral residency. They diagnose the cause of a pet's behavior problem, often in coordination with your veterinarian.

Most veterinary schools have behavior clinics or at least a behaviorist on staff. If you do not live near a vet school, some offer consultation phone lines where you can make an appointment with a behaviorist on staff to discuss the problem. There is usually a fee, and some request a video of the animal's behavior prior to the consultation. Although the fees are often steep, it is well worth the cost to be able to discuss the problem with a certified behaviorist.

Some obedience trainers and other pet professionals may be able to help with undesirable behaviors. After all, they have years of experience working with dogs and know their thought processes. As long as they use positive reinforcement and good communication, it can be a very positive experience. Just be aware of what the trainer is doing and make sure the problem is not progressing.

Working with any behavior problem takes time and patience, as well as the ability to be one step ahead of your dog. Once you start seeing an improvement in his behavior, it will all be worthwhile.

ACTIVITIES
WITH YOUR
SHIH TZU

AX, OTCH, RAE, CD, RN, UDX, CGC—these letters may look as if they came from a bowl of alphabet soup, but they are actually just a few of the titles your Shih Tzu can earn doing organized sports. Or, if sports aren't for you, you and your dog may enjoy visiting nursing homes or showing classrooms of adoring children how to raise a good canine citizen. There are numerous fun things you can do to spend time with your Shih Tzu and take advantage of the many positive qualities this breed has to offer.

DOG SHOWS (CONFORMATION)

If you bought your Shih Tzu to show, you are most likely working closely with your breeder to learn the art of training, grooming, and presenting your dog. Here is a brief overview of what the world of conformation showing has to offer.

American Kennel Club (AKC) dog shows draw more than three million entries annually. Conformation events are intended to evaluate breeding stock. The dog's overall appearance and structure are an indication of the dog's ability to produce quality puppies. The judges examine each dog to see whether the teeth, muscles, bones, and coat texture conform to the breed's standard. They view each dog in profile for overall balance and watch each dog move to see how all of those features fit together in action.

The dogs do not actually compete against each other. They are judged by how closely they meet the breed standard. That is, how closely each dog compares to the judge's mental image of the "perfect" dog. This is where championship titles are earned.

At conformation shows, dogs are judged by how closely they meet the breed standard.

There are several types of conformation shows.

- All-breed shows offer competitions for more than 150 breeds and varieties of dogs recognized by the AKC.
- Specialty shows are restricted to dogs of a specific breed, such as the one held annually by the American Shih Tzu Club.
- Group shows are limited to dogs belonging to one of the seven groups (Sporting, Hound, Working, Terrier, Toy, Non-Sporting, and Herding).

In order to be eligible to compete, your Shih Tzu must be AKC registered (but not on a Limited Registration) and at least six months old. Spayed or neutered dogs are not eligible to compete in conformation classes. The closer your dog is to the breed standard, the better chance he will have of doing well.

Junior Showmanship is offered for children 9 to 18 years of age. The dogs are not judged, but instead the juniors are judged on how skillfully they present their dogs. This is an excellent way to introduce your child into the wonderful competitive world of dogs and help your youngster build confidence and poise.

ATTENDING A DOG SHOW

If you decide to attend a dog show, there are a few things to remember.
- Do not take your Shih Tzu with you to the show. (Unentered dogs typically are not allowed on the premises.)
- Do not pet a dog without asking for permission. The dog may have just been groomed and made ready to go into the show ring.
- Visit the information booths for health tips, nutrition advice, etc. And don't forget to visit the vendors to buy a new toy for your Shih Tzu.
- Take a chair or arrive early, as seating is usually limited.
- If you are considering getting a purebred dog, talk to the breeders and exhibitors of that breed, as they are the experts on the breed. Talk to them after they have finished showing, since beforehand they will be concentrating on getting into the ring.
- Some shows prohibit baby strollers because of crowded conditions at ringside and to protect the dogs from being bumped. If you take your young child, be careful that the child does not grab or poke the dogs within reach.

Check out the AKC website (www.akc.org) to see what shows are coming up in your area.

PERFORMANCE EVENTS

The AKC offers obedience, agility, herding, and field trials; rally; lure coursing; hunting and tracking tests; and coonhound and earth dog events. Shih Tzu are not eligible to compete in herding trials, field trials, lure coursing, hunting trials, and earth dog events, as those are offered only for certain breeds.

These events are exciting to watch and are being covered more and more often on television. To participate, a dog does not have to be "conformation" quality, can be spayed or neutered, and does not have to be in show coat—he just has to have fun. These types of events allow an owner to showcase the dog's natural instincts and talents.

Many kennel clubs, obedience clubs, and individuals offer classes that help you provide training in the required exercises and understand the regulations that apply when you are competing.

While excellent in performance events, some Shih Tzu find it necessary to greet the judge in the middle of an exercise—or take a shortcut through the course that makes more sense to them! They love to show how clever they are. But once your dog learns the ropes and realizes how happy he can make you, he can excel at just about anything and make you proud.

REGISTRATION REQUIREMENTS

To compete, your Shih Tzu must be registered with the AKC, but he may compete with a Limited Registration. This is a stipulation set by the dog's breeder and means the dog is registered but that no litters produced by that dog are eligible for registration. Dogs of any breed recognized by the AKC who do not have registration papers or known parents may qualify for a Purebred Alternative Listing/Indefinite Listing Privilege (PAL/ILP). This makes the dog eligible to participate in performance events. Photos are required to prove the dog is a registerable breed. The dog must be spayed or neutered.

The AKC Canine Partners program now allows mixed-breed dogs or dogs ineligible for AKC registration to compete in events such as obedience, rally, and agility. These dogs also must be spayed or neutered.

AGILITY

The fastest-growing dog sport in the United States, agility trials are as much fun for the spectators as they are for the dog and his owner. Here the dog demonstrates his versatility by following cues from the handler through a timed obstacle course of jumps, tunnels, weave poles, and other objects. This activity provides fun and exercise for both dog and handler.

Agility is a time and fault sport where the qualifying requirements are more challenging as the competition class levels get higher. There are two types of faults: time and penalty. Time faults are given for every second a dog goes over the Standard Course Time. Some of the penalty faults are taking an obstacle out

Agility is a timed obstacle course of jumps, tunnels, weave poles, and other objects.

of sequence, displacing a bar or panel on a jump, or exceeding the amount of time set by the judge for running the course.

Classes are divided by jump heights in order to make the competition equal among the different sizes of dogs.

The classes offered at an agility trial are:

• Standard: contact obstacles include an A-frame, dog walk, and seesaw as well as jumps, weave poles, a pause table, tunnels, and a closed tunnel.

• Jumpers with Weaves: a very fast course requiring instant decisions by the handler and close attention from the dog.

• Fifteen And Send Time (FAST): an additional test of strategy, skill, accuracy, speed, timing and distance handling, to demonstrate a dog's athletic ability and willingness to work with his handler

Shih Tzu are fun-loving and nimble enough to excel at musical freestyle.

A perfect score in any class at any level is 100, with a minimum score of 85, except in the Excellent B class, where the minimum score is 100. A dog must earn three qualifying scores under two different judges for a title. The minimum time allowed to run the course and the number of obstacles to complete successfully increase as the level of difficulty increases. There are three levels for each class: Novice, Open, and Excellent. In the Excellent B level the dog/handler teams can earn the title of Master Agility Champion (MACH).

MUSICAL FREESTYLE: DANCING WITH THE (DOG) STARS

You and your Shih Tzu could be dancing with the stars!

Musical freestyle combines dog obedience and dance, with the handler and dog performing dance-oriented footwork in time to music. It can be sport focused, precision focused, or performance focused depending on personalities, goals, and teamwork.

Organizers of the sport joined to share an interest in more creative obedience demonstrations, a love of music, and inspiration from

PUPPY POINTER

Just about every activity you do with your dog requires some basic obedience, even taking him for a walk. Start your puppy out right by teaching him basic commands such as *sit, stay, heel,* and *come.*

an equine sport called musical freestyle, a form of dressage. The first musical freestyle group, Musical Canine Sports International, was founded in British Columbia, Canada, in 1991.

Another well-known form of this sport is Canine Freestyle, a choreographed performance organized with music. Every movement is accomplished through the use of verbal cues and body language. The emphasis is always on the dog. This sport is competitive and has four performance levels.

OBEDIENCE

Obedience is a very popular sport you can enjoy with your Shih Tzu. At an obedience trial the dog and his handler (you) are judged on how closely the two of you match the judge's mental picture of a theoretically perfect performance as you execute a series of specified exercises.

Obedience trials in the United States date back to 1933. The original concept behind obedience training was to develop a very close working relationship between human beings and dogs, while demonstrating the usefulness and enthusiasm of dogs. While trials have become much more specific since then, this concept still remains important today.

Obedience trials have three levels:

- Novice: includes heel, stand for exam, figure 8, recall, long sit, and long down.
- Open: includes the same exercises as Novice, plus drop on recall, retrieve, high jump, and broad jump, adjusted to breed requirements.
- Utility: tests the dog's skills even further with signal exercises, scent discrimination, and directed retrieve of an object.

A dog receives a qualifying score when he earns more than 50 percent of the points for each exercise, with a total of at least 170 points out of 200. Each of these qualifications is called a "leg," and you and your dog must earn three legs for a title, such as Companion Dog (CD), Companion Dog Excellent (CDX), Utility Dog (UD), and Utility Dog Excellent (UDX). More advanced dogs and handlers can go on to an Obedience Trial Championship (OTCH) and the National Obedience Champion (NOC), awarded annually to the dog that wins the AKC National Obedience Invitational.

An interesting side note—the person handling the dog is judged just as much as the dog is. Handler errors are penalized as much as any mistakes the dog makes.

RALLY

Rally (or rally obedience) was designed with the traditional pet owner in mind, but it can also be enjoyed at higher levels of competition. A dog trained in rally will tend to behave in the home, in public places, and in the presence of other dogs.

The dog and handler team completes a course that has been designed by the rally judge. The team moves at its own pace, very similar to rally-style auto racing. There are three levels: Novice, Advanced and Excellent. In Novice rally, the judge tells the team to begin, and the team moves continuously at a brisk but normal pace with the dog under control at the handler's left side. The team will reach sign posts at which they will be asked to perform tasks such as *sit*, *stay*, *down*, *come*, and *heel*. In Advanced rally, at least one jump is added, and in rally Excellent, the work is done off leash on a course that includes at least one jump and demonstrates more precise skill and coordination. The judge watches for a smooth performance as well as skill in following the directions at each station. Scoring is not as strict as traditional obedience.

In rally, a dog and handler complete a course that has been designed by a judge.

Teamwork between the dog and handler is essential. Unless otherwise specified, handlers are permitted to talk, praise, encourage, clap their hands, pat their legs, or use any verbal means of encouragement. Each performance is timed, but times are counted only if two dogs earn the same score. All dogs and handlers begin with a perfect 100. A dog and handler team is awarded a qualifying score if it retains at least 70 points after the course has been completed. Titles are Rally Novice (RN), Rally Advanced (RA), Rally Excellent (RE) and Rally Advanced Excellent (RAE).

TRACKING

Yes, a Shih Tzu can track! All dogs have a natural ability to follow a scent—after all, their sense of smell is 100,000 times greater than ours. In this event, the dog is totally in charge and the test, designed to evaluate a dog's ability to follow a trail by scent, is scored a pass or fail. The dog, who is on lead, must follow the path and find articles left on the track by a track layer. The handler must show all the articles to the judges at the end of the track. Some of the most difficult tests challenge a dog to follow human scent across various surfaces and through changing conditions. If he succeeds, he earns the tracking title for the level at which he is exhibiting.

A dog can earn three AKC Tracking titles, each with an increased degree of difficulty: the Tracking Dog (TD) title, the Tracking Dog Excellent (TDX), and the Variable Surface Tracker (VST) title. A Champion Tracker (CT), a very elite title, is awarded only to those dogs who have earned all three of the other tracking titles.

OTHER ACTIVITIES

If competition is not for you, there are still plenty of fun and rewarding things you can do with your Shih Tzu. The activities listed here are just a few of the ones you can share with your Shih Tzu. If you don't see one that's right for you, consider dog yoga, camping trips, flyball competitions—and of course, Halloween costume contests. The sky's the limit with your Shih Tzu!

CANINE GOOD CITIZEN

The AKC's Canine Good Citizen (CGC) Program is designed to reward dogs with good manners at home and in the community. Kennel clubs and obedience clubs often give the CGC Test in conjunction with shows and matches, or at special club-related events. Items on the test, all performed on leash, include:

- Accepting a friendly stranger
- Sitting politely for petting
- Appearance and grooming
- Out for a walk (walking on a loose leash)

A CGC dog shows good manners at home and out in the community.

Dog Tale

A Dog's Life: A Dogamentary™ is a hilarious and poignant documentary that explores the positive effects of the intense bond between dogs and humans, as told by Emmy-award-winning filmmaker Gayle Kirschenbaum and her Shih Tzu, Chelsea. Chelsea, rigged with a "doggie cam," hits the streets of New York with Gayle, both looking for love. But the tragic events of 9/11 alter their quest and we watch Chelsea find her true calling as a therapy dog, finding love through healing others.

- Walking through a crowd
- *Sit* and *down* on command and staying in place
- Coming when called
- Reaction to another dog
- Reaction to distraction
- Supervised separation

You may praise, encourage, and even pet the dog between exercises. Any dog who growls, snaps, bites, attacks, or attempts to attack a person or another dog is not a good citizen and is dismissed from the test. Dogs who pass the test receive a certificate from the AKC and are recorded in the Canine Good Citizen Archive.

Participating in the CGC Program is an easy and rewarding experience for you and your Shih Tzu.

SERVICE DOGS

Service dogs are legally defined by the Americans With Disabilities Act and are trained to meet the needs of their handlers who have disabilities. Federal laws protect the rights of individuals with disabilities to be accompanied by their service animals in public places. Service animals are not considered pets.

The most well-known type of service dog is the Seeing Eye dog, an occupation reserved for larger dog breeds. However, there are other services a small dog like a Shih Tzu can provide. The psychiatric service dog, a relatively new breed of service animal, works to lessen a handler's psychiatric disabilities, such as anxiety disorder, depression, or post- traumatic stress disorder.

Small dogs are also trained to assist deaf people with varying degrees of impairment. The dogs alert their owners to a variety of sounds, usually by coming up to the person and going back to the source of the sound. They will signal a doorbell, phone, smoke alarm, a crying baby, and much more. Other service dogs alert the owner if their insulin levels are low or if an epileptic seizure is imminent. In the United States, service dogs enjoy the same rights of access as guide dogs and are permitted anywhere.

THERAPY DOGS

What better therapy for a hospital or nursing home patient than a friendly, happy Shih Tzu, eager to make a new friend? There are several ways to become eligible for a therapy dog program.

Therapy animals are not defined by federal law, but some states have laws defining therapy animals. The animals are usually the handler's personal pets. You may be able to have your dog certified as a therapy dog locally, or you can work with national organizations. Generally speaking, a dog must be trained on basic commands (*sit*, *down*, *stay*), to walk politely on leash, not show aggressive behaviors, and remain calm in unfamiliar settings such as hospitals, nursing homes, and schools. Some also require that a dog complete some obedience training classes before he can be evaluated.

Therapy Dogs International

Therapy Dogs International (TDI) has registered more than 21,000 dog/handler teams for the purpose of visiting nursing homes, hospitals, and other institutions. TDI is dedicated to the regulating, testing, and registration of therapy dogs and their volunteer handlers.

In order to become a therapy dog, your Shih Tzu must be tested and evaluated by a Certified TDI Evaluator. The dog must be a minimum of one year of age and have a sound temperament. Each dog must pass a temperament evaluation for suitability, such as the AKC's CGC. The test will also evaluate the dog's behavior around people using some type of service equipment (wheelchairs, crutches, etc.).

Shih Tzu make wonderful therapy dogs.

The dogs and their humans can take part in a number of activities, including visits to hospitals, nursing homes, shelters, and assisted living communities. At hospice facilities, Therapy Dogs assist people with the grieving process. Sometimes loved ones get to know a Therapy Dog team because of their visits during a patient's final stages of life, and families often request that the dog/handler team come to the funeral home for added support.

TDI's Children Reading to Dogs program (Tail Waggin' Tutors) provides a relaxed and "dog-friendly" atmosphere where students practice the skill of reading. Many of the children chosen for this program have difficulties reading and have developed self-esteem issues, or they are self-conscious when reading aloud in front of other classmates. Reading to dogs has been shown to increase self-esteem and nurture an interest in reading.

TDI members and their therapy dogs have also provided some unconditional love in the form of disaster relief in Oklahoma City in the aftermath of the destruction of the Alfred P. Murrah Federal Building as well as after September 11, 2001. They were present in Baton Rouge, Louisiana, to provide stress relief for refugees and the rescue workers coming to and from New Orleans in the aftermath of Hurricane Katrina.

Delta Society

The Delta Society established Pet Partners in 1990 to train volunteers and their pets to visit hospitals, nursing homes, rehabilitation centers, schools, and other facilities. Pet Partners is the only national registry that requires volunteer training and screening of animal-handler teams. The national network links volunteers with facilities in their own communities that request visiting pets and helps Pet Partners contact facilities to begin visits in new locations.

TRAVELING WITH YOUR SHIH TZU

Because of the Shih Tzu's portable size, traveling with him is easy. Even crates and bags designed for car and air travel are small and compact.

BY CAR

A crate or dog airline bag is the safest way to transport your dog in your car. A canine car seat will work as long as it totally restrains your dog. The goal is to keep him from jumping on you while you are driving. And in the case of an accident, you don't want him to be thrown from the car and become injured or run away. Remember, it is not safe to hold a dog on your lap in the car, particularly when you are in a seat protected by air bags. If your car has front seat air bags, keep the dog secured in the back seat.

If your dog has a tendency to become carsick, ask your vet about anti-nausea medication, and don't feed him the morning of your trip.

Car window shades near where you keep the crate or bag can help keep the area cool in warm weather. Of course, never leave your dog in the car, especially when it is warm outside. It takes only minutes for a pet to succumb to heatstroke and suffocation. If there is no way around leaving your pet in the car, leave him at home.

When traveling by car, don't forget food and water, and some basic grooming tools if you will be gone for a few days. Some "waterless shampoo" could also come in handy. Your dog's favorite

A canine car harness or restraint will keep your Shih Tzu safe while traveling.

toy will be much appreciated when he starts to get bored. Make provisions for picking up poop at rest stops—carry sandwich bags or other bags for pick-up and dispose of them properly.

It is a good idea to have some information about your dog attached to the crate in case of an accident. For example, your name, address, phone numbers, and e-mail, and any pertinent medical information about your dog. In a worst case scenario, you should have a contact person to speak for the dog if you are unable to.

BY AIR

Luckily, a Shih Tzu is small enough to travel with you in the cabin if you fly. Consult the airline about approved carry-on bags. Have your dog's leash and collar easily accessible for walking prior to departure, and make sure he has his identification tags on and is microchipped. Tape any essential information on his travel kennel, including his name, home address, destination address, and phone number, and any medication he may need.

Don't sedate him, because this can affect his respiratory and/or cardiovascular function, as well as his ability to maintain equilibrium if he is jostled around. Some airlines will not accept sedated pets at all.

A health certificate and rabies vaccination are required for all dogs for travel abroad and for returning to the United States. Check with your vet for the complete range of vaccinations required and with the airline and country to which you're heading.

LODGING

Before you make your hotel, motel, or cabin reservations, be sure to ask what the policy is about pets. Some do not allow pets at all, some allow one small pet, and others allow any pet but may require a damage deposit.

In order for your dog to be a good canine guest, keep him in his crate while you are out of the room so he will be safe when the housekeeping staff comes to clean. Have plastic bags for cleanup and some carpet cleaner just in case. You won't want to leave your dog alone, even in the crate, if he will bark. This indicates your dog is stressed or afraid, and it will disturb other guests.

PET SITTERS

If it is simply impossible to take your Shih Tzu with you on a trip, and you would prefer he not stay in a boarding kennel, consider a pet sitter. These professionals stay at your house while you are away or come in several times per day to take care of your dog. Pets are happier and less stressed at home, and their exposure to illness is minimized.

Some pet sitters offer services such as dog walking, pooper-scooping, and errand services. If you are unable to run your dog to the vet, your dog sitter can help out there as well. It is not uncommon for the pet sitter to become an invaluable member of the pet's family.

You'll be surprised just how many places you can go with your Shih Tzu.

RESOURCES

ASSOCIATIONS AND ORGANIZATIONS

BREED CLUBS

American Kennel Club (AKC)
5580 Centerview Drive
Raleigh, NC 27606
Telephone: (919) 233-9767
Fax: (919) 233-3627
E-Mail: info@akc.org
www.akc.org

American Shih Tzu Club, Inc. (ASTC)
www.americanshihtzuclub.org

Canadian Kennel Club (CKC)
89 Skyway Avenue, Suite 100
Etobicoke, Ontario M9W 6R4
Telephone: (416) 675-5511
Fax: (416) 675-6506
E-Mail: information@ckc.ca
www.ckc.ca

Federation Cynologique Internationale (FCI)
Secretariat General de la FCI
Place Albert 1er, 13
B – 6530 Thuin
Belqique
www.fci.be

The Kennel Club
1 Clarges Street
London
W1J 8AB
Telephone: 0870 606 6750
Fax: 0207 518 1058
www.the-kennel-club.org.uk

United Kennel Club (UKC)
100 E. Kilgore Road
Kalamazoo, MI 49002-5584
Telephone: (269) 343-9020
Fax: (269) 343-7037
E-Mail: pbickell@ukcdogs.com
www.ukcdogs.com

PET SITTERS

National Association of Professional Pet Sitters
15000 Commerce Parkway, Suite C
Mt. Laurel, NJ 08054
Telephone: (856) 439-0324
Fax: (856) 439-0525
E-Mail: napps@ahint.com
www.petsitters.org

Pet Sitters International
201 East King Street
King, NC 27021-9161
Telephone: (336) 983-9222
Fax: (336) 983-5266
E-Mail: info@petsit.com
www.petsit.com

Rescue Organizations and Animal Welfare Groups
American Humane Association (AHA)
63 Inverness Drive East
Englewood, CO 80112
Telephone: (303) 792-9900
Fax: (303) 792-5333
www.americanhumane.org

American Society for the Prevention of Cruelty to Animals (ASPCA)
424 E. 92nd Street
New York, NY 10128-6804
Telephone: (212) 876-7700
www.aspca.org

Royal Society for the Prevention of Cruelty to Animals (RSPCA)
RSPCA Enquiries Service
Wilberforce Way, Southwater,
Horsham, West Sussex RH13 9RS
United Kingdom
Telephone: 0870 3335 999
Fax: 0870 7530 284
www.rspca.org.uk

SPORTS

International Agility Link (IAL)
Global Administrator: Steve Drinkwater
E-Mail: yunde@powerup.au
www.agilityclick.com/~ial

The World Canine Freestyle Organization, Inc.
P.O. Box 350122
Brooklyn, NY 11235
Telephone: (718) 332-8336
Fax: (718) 646-2686
E-Mail: WCFODOGS@aol.com
www.worldcaninefreestyle.org

THERAPY

Delta Society
875 124th Ave, NE, Suite 101
Bellevue, WA 98005
Telephone: (425) 679-5500
Fax: (425) 679-5539
E-Mail: info@DeltaSociety.org
www.deltasociety.org

Therapy Dogs Inc.
P.O. Box 20227
Cheyenne WY 82003
Telephone: (877) 843-7364
Fax: (307) 638-2079
E-Mail: therapydogsinc@qwestoffice.net
www.therapydogs.com

Therapy Dogs International (TDI)
88 Bartley Road
Flanders, NJ 07836
Telephone: (973) 252-9800
Fax: (973) 252-7171
E-Mail: tdi@gti.net
www.tdi-dog.org

TRAINING

Association of Pet Dog Trainers
(APDT)
150 Executive Center Drive Box 35
Greenville, SC 29615
Telephone: (800) PET-DOGS
Fax: (864) 331-0767
E-Mail: information@apdt.com
www.apdt.com

International Association of
Animal Behavior Consultants
(IAABC)
565 Callery Road
Cranberry Township, PA 16066
E-Mail: info@iaabc.org
www.iaabc.org

National Association of Dog
Obedience Instructors (NADOI)
PMB 369
729 Grapevine Highway
Hurst, TX 76054-2085
www.nadoi.org

VETERINARY AND HEALTH RESOURCES

Academy of Veterinary
Homeopathy (AVH)
P.O. Box 9280
Wilmington, DE 19809
Telephone: (866) 652-1590
Fax: (866) 652-1590
www.theavh.org

American Academy of Veterinary
Acupuncture (AAVA)
P.O. Box 1058
Glastonbury, CT 06033
Telephone: (860) 632-9911
Fax: (860) 659-8772
www.aava.org

American Animal Hospital
Association (AAHA)
12575 W. Bayaud Ave.
Lakewood, CO 80228
Telephone: (303) 986-2800
Fax: (303) 986-1700
E-Mail: info@aahanet.org
www.aahanet.org

American College of Veterinary
Internal Medicine (ACVIM)
1997 Wadsworth Blvd., Suite A
Lakewood, CO 80214-5293
Telephone: (800) 245-9081
Fax: (303) 231-0880
Email: ACVIM@ACVIM.org
www.acvim.org

American College of Veterinary
Ophthalmologists (ACVO)
P.O. Box 1311
Meridian, ID 83860
Telephone: (208) 466-7624
Fax: (208) 466-7693
E-Mail: office09@acvo.com
www.acvo.com

American Holistic Veterinary
Medical Association (AHVMA)
2218 Old Emmorton Road
Bel Air, MD 21015
Telephone: (410) 569-0795
Fax: (410) 569-2346
E-Mail: office@ahvma.org
www.ahvma.org

American Veterinary Medical
Association (AVMA)
1931 North Meacham Road, Suite
100
Schaumburg, IL 60173-4360
Telephone: (847) 925-8070
Fax: (847) 925-1329
E-Mail: avmainfo@avma.org
www.avma.org

ASPCA Animal Poison Control
Center
Telephone: (888) 426-4435
www.aspca.org

British Veterinary Association
(BVA)
7 Mansfield Street
London
W1G 9NQ
Telephone: 0207 636 6541
Fax: 0207 908 6349
E-Mail: bvahq@bva.co.uk
www.bva.co.uk

Canine Eye Registration
Foundation (CERF)
VMDB/CERF
1717 Philo Road
P O Box 3007
Urbana, IL 61803-3007
Telephone: (217) 693-4800
Fax: (217) 693-4801
E-Mail: CERF@vmbd.org
www.vmdb.org

Orthopedic Foundation for
Animals (OFA)
2300 NE Nifong Blvd
Columbus, MO 65201-3856
Telephone: (573) 442-0418
Fax: (573) 875-5073
Email: ofa@offa.org
www.offa.org

US Food and Drug Administration Center for Veterinary Medicine (CVM)

7519 Standish Place

HFV-12

Rockville, MD 20855-0001

Telephone: (240) 276-9300 or (888) INFO-FDA

www.fda.gov/cvm

REFERENCES
BOOKS AND JOURNALS

Beaver, Bonnie. *Canine Behavior: A Guide for Veterinarians*. Philadelphia: W.B. Saunders, 1999.

Bovsun, Mara. "Puddle Jumping." *AKC Gazette*. April 2009, 32-35.

Burch, Mary, Ph.D., and Jon S. Bailey, Ph.D. *How Dogs Learn*. New York: Howell Book House, 1999.

Collier, V.W. F. *Dogs of China and Japan in Nature and Art*. New York: Frederick A. Stokes Company Publishers, 1921.

Estep, Daniel Q., Ph.D., and Suzanne Hetts, Ph.D. *Help! I'm Barking and I Can't Be Quiet*. Littleton, Colorado: Island Dog Press, 2004.

Goldston, Richard T., DVM, and Johnny D, Hoskins, DVM, PhD. *Geriatrics & Gerontology of the Dog and Cat*. Philadelphia: W.B. Saunders Company, 1995.

Joris, Victor. *The Complete Shih Tzu*. New York: Howell Book House, 1994.

Lange, Karen E. "Wolf to Woof: The Evolution of Dogs." *National Geographic*. January 2002, 2-31.

Legl-Jacobsson, Elisabeth. *East Asiatic Breeds*. Sweden: TryckProduktion, 1978.

Miller, Pat. *The Power of Positive Dog Training*. New York: Howell Book House, 2001.

Morgan, Patrick. "What is a Lhasa Lion Dog?" This article was printed in *Town & Country* and is from an undated clipping from the mid 1930s.

Oechtering, Gerhard U., DVM. "Brachycephalic Airway Syndrome: Successful Anesthesia and Recovery." *The North American Veterinary Conference*. 2008, 1454-1455.

Parker, Heidi G., et al. "Genetic Structure of the Purebred Domestic Dog." *Science*. 21 May 2004, 1160-1164.

Plunkett, Nancy. *A New Owner's Guide to Lhasa Apsos*. Neptune City, N.J.: T.F.H. Publications, Inc., 1998.

Quigley, Dorothy A. *The Quigley Book of the Pekingese*. New York: Howell Book House, 1964.

Ricketts, Viva Leone. *All About Toy Dogs*. New York: Howell Book House, 1972.

Riddle, Maxwell. *Dogs Through History*. Fairfax, Va.: Denlinger's Publishers, Ltd., 1987.

Rugh, Karla S., DVM, Ph.D. "Teeth." *Dog Fancy*. February 2010, pp. 29-31.

Schoen, Allen M., DVM, and Susan G. Wynn, DVM. *Complementary and Alternative Veterinary Medicine: Principles and Practice*. St. Louis: Mosby, 1998.

Seranne, Ann and Lisa M. Miller. *The Joy of Owning a Shih Tzu*. New York: Howell Book House, 1982.

Simsova, Sylva. *Tibetan and Related Dog Breeds: A Guide to Their History*. Published by the Tibetan Terrier Association, Welwyn, Hertfordshire, England, 1979.

Slatter, Douglas, Ph.D. *Fundamentals of Veterinary Ophthalmology*. Philadelphia: W.B. Saunders, 1990.

Thurston, Mary Elizabeth. *The Lost History of the Canine Race*. New York: Avon Books, 1996.

Wendt, Lloyd M. Dogs: *A Historical Journey*. New York: Howell Book House, 1996.

White, Jo Ann. "Shih Tzu Eyes." *AKC Gazette*, Shih Tzu column, March 2010, 56.

WEBSITES

About.com: Veterinary Medicine. 2010. <http://vetmedicine.about.com> (August 2010).

Adamson, Eve. "Shih Tzu: A Temperament Made for Companionship." Dummies.com. Wiley Publishing, Inc. 2010. <http://www.dummies.com/how-to/content/shih-tzu-a-temperament-made-for-companionship.html#ixzz0vfSFc61E> (July 2010).

American Kennel Club. 2010. <http://www.akc.org/> (June 2010).

The American Pet Products Association. 2010. <http://www.americanpetproducts.org/> (August 2010).

American Shih Tzu Club. 2009. <http://americanshihtzuclub.org/> (June 2010).

American Veterinary Medical Association. 2010. < http://www.avma.org/>. (July, August 2010)

American Society for the Prevention of Cruelty to Animals. 2010. <http://www.aspca.org/>. (August 2010)

"Brief History of Dog Food, A." Terrierman's Daily Dose. August 09, 2008. ‹http://terriermandotcom.blogspot.com/2004/09/history-of-dog-food.html› (August 2010).

Delta Society. 2010. ‹http://www.deltasociety.org› (August 2010).

Derr, Mark. "Collie or Pug? Study Finds the Genetic Code." New York Times. 21 May 2004. ‹http://www.nytimes.com/2004/05/21/science/21dog.html?ex=1400472000&en=6b49c839cde80d81&ei=5007&partner=USERLAND› (July 2010).

"Food and Nutrition." Dog Time. 2009. ‹http://dogtime.com/food-nutrition.html› (August 2010).

Marien-de Luca, Catherine. Shih Tzu (Lhasa Lion Dog). Dog Breeds of the World. 2004-2010. ‹http://dogbreeds.bulldoginformation.com/shih-tzu.html› (August 5, 2010).

Muns, Margaret, DVM. "Practical Canine Nutrition." Best Friends Animal Sanctuary. 2010. ‹http://www.bestfriends.org/› (August 2010).

PetEducation.com. ‹http://www.peteducation.com› (August 2010).

PetPlace.com. Intelligent Content Corp. 2010. ‹ http://www.petplace.com/dogs/› (August 2010).

"Pets in Hot Cars." Partnership for Animal Welfare. ‹http://www.paw-rescue.org/› (August 2010).

"Portosystemic Shunts." The University of Tennessee Institute of Agriculture. ‹http://www.vet.utk.edu/clinical/sacs/shunt/faq.php› (August 2010).

Pryor, Karen. Clicker Training. 2010. ‹ http://www.clickertraining.com/› (August 2010).

"Shih Tzu." All Small Dog Breeds. 2006 to 2009. ‹http://www.allsmalldogbreeds.com/shih-tzu.html› (July 2010).

Therapy Dogs International. 2010. ‹ http://www.tdi-dog.org/› (August 2010).

"Which Came First - Tibetan Spaniels or Pekingese?" Tibetan Spaniel Network. 2010. ‹http://www.tibbie.net/tibbies-first.html Tibetan Spaniel Network› (July 2010).

"Top Pet Industry Trends for 2009." Pawsible Marketing. Jan. 19, 2009. ‹http://www.marketingmypetbusiness.com/› (August 2010).

"Dog Genome Researchers Track Paw Prints of Selective Breeding." Science Daily. 19 January 2010. ‹http://www.sciencedaily.com/releases/2010/01/100113172357.htm› (July 2010).

Vetinfo. 2010. ‹ttp://www.vetinfo.com/› (August 2010).

Virbac Animal Health. 2010. ‹http://www.virbacvet.com/news/article/1012/› (August 2010).

WebMed. 2010. ‹http://pets.webmd.com/dogs/ › (August 2010).

Taking the Bite out of Fleas and Ticks." U.S. Department of Health & Human Services. October 2001. ‹www.fda.gov›

INDEX

Note: Boldfaced numbers indicate illustrations.

PHOTO CREDITS

DEDICATION

This book is dedicated to my first Lhasa Apso, Barney, who made me fall in love with and appreciate all of the Tibetan breeds.

ACKNOWLEDGMENTS

I would like to thank the following people for submitting photos for this book:

Phyllis Ensley, Pet Action Shots, Canton, Georgia

Pat Keen, Hylan Sho Tru Show Dogs, Knightsen, California

Jan Sammons, Stars End Shih Tzu, Powder Springs, Georgia

Rita Scarberry, Louisa, Kentucky

Many thanks to Charles Drastura, Alice Kane, Pamela Rightmyer, Jan Sammons, and Rita Scarberry for their proofing skills and suggestions.

ABOUT THE AUTHOR

Jenny Drastura and her husband, Charlie, have been involved with Lhasa Apsos, Tibetan Terriers, and Maltese since 1984 when their first Lhasa, Kashi VII, C.D., aka Barney, came into their lives. While showing Barney in obedience, they caught the show bug and obtained their first conformation Lhasas from the Orlane line. The Drasturas are also very involved in rescue, particularly adoption and transport. They currently live with an assortment of Lhasa Apsos, Maltese, and rescues.

Jenny was co-editor and primary writer for The *Lhasa Apso Reporter*, a popular bi-monthly breed magazine published in the 1990s. She has been a member of the Dog Writers Association of America since 1988 and a member of the Society of Professional Journalists. She also belongs to the American Lhasa Apso Club, the American Maltese Association, the Huntington Kennel Club, and New Hope Animal Rescue Group.

As a freelance writer, Jenny has contributed articles to *Dog World* and *The AKC Gazette*, as well as numerous breed publications. Her short story, "Kanda's Return," was published in *God's Messengers: What Animals Teach Us About the Divine.*

Jenny has a master of arts degree in journalism and has been with Marshall University in Huntington, West Virginia, in various writing capacities for the past 20 years. She is editor of the alumni magazine for Marshall's Joan C. Edwards School of Medicine.

ABOUT ANIMAL PLANET™

Animal Planet™ is the only television network dedicated exclusively to the connection between humans and animals. The network brings people of all ages together by tapping into our fundamental fascination with animals through an array of fresh programming that includes humor, competition, drama, and spectacle from the animal kingdom.

ABOUT *DOGS 101*

The most comprehensive—and most endearing—dog encyclopedia on television, *DOGS 101* spotlights the adorable, the feisty and the unexpected. A wide-ranging rundown of everyone's favorite dog breeds—from the Dalmatian to Xoloitzcuintli —this series surveys a variety of breeds for their behavioral quirks, genetic history, most famous examples and wildest trivia. Learn which dogs are best for urban living and which would be the best fit for your family. Using a mix of animal experts, pop-culture footage and stylized dog photography, *DOGS 101* is an unprecedented look at man's best friend.